Resolving Behaviour Problems in Your School

Resolving Behaviour Problems in Your School

A Practical Guide for Teachers and Support Staff

Chris Lee

P·C·P

Paul Chapman
Publishing

First published 2007

Paul Chapman Publishing
A SAGE Publications Company
1 Oliver's Yard
55 City Road
London EC1Y 1SP

SAGE Publications Inc
2455 Teller Road
Thousand Oaks, California 91320

SAGE Publications India Pvt Ltd
B 1/I 1, Mohan Cooperative Industrial Area
Mathura Road, New Delhi 110 044
India

SAGE Publications Asia-Pacific Pte Ltd
33 Pekin Street #02–01
Far East Square
Singapore 048763

Library of Congress Control Number: 2007920531

A catalogue record for this book is available from the British Library

ISBN-978-1-4129-2413-9
ISBN-978-1-4129-2414-6 (pbk)

Typeset by Pantek Arts Ltd, Maidstone, Kent
Printed in Great Britain by Cromwell Press Ltd, Trowbridge, Wiltshire
Printed on paper from sustainable resources

Contents

List of staff development exercises

Acknowledgements

I am indebted to all those who have supported me in writing this book, especially Liz, Nick and Ben. I should like to dedicate it to all the teachers, teaching assistants and other school staff who have worked with me in professional development sessions and who have informed and helped to develop the ideas herein. Special thanks go to Teri-Anne, Jeff, Carolyn and Maureen.

About the author

Dr Chris Lee is Head of the School of Continuing Professional Development at the University of Plymouth. His main researching and lecturing foci are bullying and behaviour management. Prior to his career in higher education he taught in both secondary and special schools.

Foreword

In this book Chris Lee clearly demonstrates his wide experience and knowledge in behaviour leadership and behaviour concerns in schools.

The concepts, practices, skills and policy guidelines are well argued and grounded in what teachers face in their day-to-day teaching. Indeed Chris always presents his arguments in light of realistic, practical, effective and humane practice.

At all times Chris Lee emphasises that no one single (or simple) argument, policy or practice can match the concerns raised about behaviour in contemporary education – particularly in the area of behaviour and discipline concerns.

A significant feature of Chris' work is the consistent emphasis on informed and reflective professional understandings that need to underpin classroom and school discipline.

This book will enable an informed policy process and practice in behaviour leadership in schools. Its emphasis on consciously informed skill and practice is enhanced by use of discussion and policy frameworks, guidelines and question formats (photocopiable).

Chris Lee's book ably balances well argued and developed theoretical *and* practical approaches to behaviour policy and practice. There is also a consistent emphasis – a crucial emphasis – on the need to develop a collegially supportive culture in the management and support of student behaviour in schools. Again Chris sets out useful, credible and practical guidelines for such support.

I commend this book to teachers and school leaders to enable an *informed*, serious and grounded review of behaviour management.

Bill Rogers

Preface

The initial idea for this book emerged from groups of teachers who were studying behaviour management issues as a modular component of their university MA studies. We talked about the need for a textbook that supported and helped them in the creation of whole school policies that addressed behavioural issues. After several conversations with these groups and other education professionals I decided to try to write the book and to retain a focus on the key areas that arose from the concerns of staff including their emphasis upon policy generation. However, with the focus on policy I am not just aiming towards the production of a document that informs, examines and enhances practice in classrooms and schools, laudable though that those ambitions are. I want to go deeper and capture the spirit of ideas and concepts that teachers, teaching assistants and other staff wrestle with in their professional development and their everyday working lives.

As part of the Masters programme mentioned above, teachers and other education professionals are required to address their studies through collecting data and analysing it, investigating and interrogating research literature, developing projects, reflecting on their practice and considering education issues through *making an argument*, not necessarily a debate, but addressing the tensions, difficulties and stances that surround most contemporary educational issues. In many ways it was the approach through argument that was both the most difficult and the most rewarding for participants as it demanded that teachers arrive at a clear personal stance on what are central concerns or topics. They did so by evaluating and reflecting upon perspectives from research literature, professional literature, the opinions of others and, most importantly, their own experiences in the classroom. So many times they embarked on their studies looking for answers as if studying education, and our focus on behaviour management issues, would elicit the 'blacks' and the 'whites'. What they found, however, was that there were no blacks and whites but simply a set of 'greys' and that through argument they could find the greys that resonated with their ideas, values and experiences and also the depths of those greys. Argument was not about opposing views and heated moments of debate and contradictions but about seeing a cause, seeing different views, making the case and understanding the reasoning behind it. It was not only finding out about theories and practices that matched personal ideologies, it was also about examining their effectiveness as successful strategies in the classroom.

Behaviour management policy includes identifying and developing skills that prevent or resolve classroom and school problems as well as staff attending courses to explore everything from the key hot tips to total solutions. So many of the thinkers in this area advocate their theories as if they are the only way forward – 'the answer' – and the documents from central government and agencies assert their latest mantras as the solution for all. This book does none of that – it advocates instead that education professionals need to be informed, make decisions, perceive the alternatives, understand the complexity and come to a solution that matches their personal professionalism. It is not a book of answers but of ideas and choices. It is not a book of quick fixes but it is one which hopefully will nurture thoughtful professional reflection that leads to consistent practice. Not all the ideas mentioned will:

- work all the time (this will depend on skills, applicability, context and class/pupil response)

- apply to your situation (age taught, school ethos, group chemistry)

- resonate with your own ideas and values as an education professional.

The book contains ideas and debates and, inevitably, some personally advocated 'greys' that are not offered as answers but have resounded with me and seem worth sharing. The aim of the book is simply to help you identify your ideas, clarify your values, improve your practice and come closer to *your* greys and know them well.

In terms of audience, it is designed for teachers, teaching assistants and any other professional staff including educational psychologists who work with pupils. Unless stated otherwise, the generic term 'staff' is used to cover the range of adults who come into contact with pupils in schools. Students undertaking training may also find useful discussion points and practices.

Finally, during a research project in a primary school I came across a group of caring and professional staff who were thoughtful about all that they did but tended to blame early afternoon disruption on the mealtime assistants/lunchtime supervisors. This group of underpaid workers are often untrained and ignored in terms of staff development. This book contains a plea for 'whole school' to mean just that – everyone working in a school. One of the main purposes of this book is to inform staff development and it must be remembered that staff include secretaries, caretakers and mealtime assistants.

How to use this book

The title of this book has two key words within it – 'resolving' and 'your'. 'Resolving' does not imply that simply by enacting ideas, theories and practice suggested in this book all problems will be resolved; rather it indicates a journey towards resolution, and practitioners in schools are fully aware that there is not a 'day of resolution' but a constant journey to secure the best learning environment for children. Resolution, in this context, is more about offering clear direction on how this might be achieved and considering the skills and processes that constitute effective policy generation and practice. It is as much about the resolution of problem behaviour as an issue at whole school level as it is about dealing with day-to-day problem behaviours and it acknowledges that classroom control is an illusion. Forcing pupils to undertake tasks and respond to orders from staff is not control but can invite resistance, and no one can truly control such complex systems as classrooms and schools. What is more important is that staff recognise they are part of the complex system and only in control of their own behaviour and their own skills and that what this brings is *influence* (Gordon, 1996). Once teachers and teaching assistants recognise how much their behaviour influences their pupils and they discard notions of 'top down' control, they can engage more positively in activities that enhance their relationships with their pupils through professional development. This book contains many such activities.

'Your' is used to suggest that not all the ideas and practices discussed in the book are applicable to you and you are encouraged to select those which best suit the culture of your school, the environment in which you work, your role within that environment, current policy and practice and your own views and opinions. It also serves to indicate that whatever approaches are adopted they need to align with your own personal and professional values since the alternative is a feeling of dislocation and the likely outcome is stress.

Chapter summary

Chapter 1 addresses some of the broad issues of constructing policy on behaviour management and how these policies relate to the practices in schools. It offers a model of a policy before suggesting a way forward in the process of devising and reviewing that policy.

Chapter 2 considers the significance of theory to effective practice in behaviour management before offering a profile of the major groups of theories on behaviour management.

Chapter 3 evaluates key issues concerning rights, rules and rewards in schools. It helps staff to engage in thinking about positive behaviour management systems and directly informs statements that can be made in a policy and the resultant practices.

Chapter 4 looks at approaches to the more negative aspect of systems when behaviour is continually disruptive and rules are broken. It provides a continuum that moves from punishment, sanctions and consequences to restorative justice approaches and, like its predecessor, directly informs statements that can be made in a policy and the consequent practices.

Chapter 5 considers what everyday practices staff can adopt to prevent disruptive behaviour in the school and classroom. It aims to inform behaviour policy statements and certainly will have an impact on the tone of a statement.

Chapter 6 considers how staff can react to classroom problems. As with all the chapters, it is underpinned by the idea that adults are powerful forces in the classroom and make a difference that is not based upon authority but upon their skills as professional practitioners.

Chapter 7 concludes with a summary of key themes and ideas linked to behaviour management issues.

Additional features

Throughout the book there are tables that analyse concepts, provide information, consider data and develop categories. The material in the tables has been drawn from analysis and reading of relevant literature, and includes extended lists of points for personal information and staff development that can be used in any way deemed fit.

STAFF DEVELOPMENT EXERCISE

Suggested activities for professional development in groups or for a whole staff are presented in shaded boxes like this one. They are called 'Staff Development Exercises' **(SDE)** and have a code linked to the chapter and the order in which they appear in that chapter. These boxes can be adapted for individual staff in their reflection on and engagement with the featured issues. The appendix at the end of the book lists the SDEs and their approximate times. They help the person planning staff development and reflection on policy and practice to select and plan a series of events.

Some activities have a twofold role in that they are designed *to feed directly into policy decisions* and they also highlight the *crucial arguments and issues* that are raised in that section. With that in mind it is essential that staff using the activities, whether individually or as part of professional development, familiarise themselves with the context and relevant chapter. In addition, it is likely that a variety of views will be encountered when undertaking the exercises and there may be heated moments which can be pre-empted through advanced recognition that they can take you into emotionally charged waters and that everyone has a right to hold a view.

There are also boxes which outline the chapter at the beginning and which draw together the key decisions that will have been made at the end of each chapter.

All the tables and activities are designed to support professional development at a variety of levels. They can be engaged with at a personal level permitting reflection and self-analysis, or at classroom level inviting teachers and teaching assistants to consider their thinking and practice. They may help inform sessions in a higher education context but *most of all* they have been designed to provide a framework for policy development at whole school level. Policy in this context does not only mean the document that encapsulates the school's approaches on matters behavioural for multiple audiences but it also means the ideals and theories that drive everyday practices in classrooms and the principles that inform them. It is then identifiable beyond statements in writing.

Main themes and ideas

There are five ideas that underpin the ideas set out in the book.

1   **Behaviour management is complex** Behaviour management in schools is a highly complex matter. It is not simply about dealing with difficult pupil behaviour but is a way in which pupils and staff can develop positive relationships that facilitate full participation in school – for all parties – and enhance learning. There are no instant fixes, simple remedies or 'magic bullets' contained within – if there were you could file it under 'fiction' – but there are suggestions linked to ideas and theories.

2   **The focus for change is on staff** The focus is on staff, teachers, teaching assistants and support staff, and their responses to pupils. It is therefore about developing policy and practice *within the school* and, although it is impossible not to consider parents by implication, classroom and school interaction remain the foci. What the book seeks to do is address the areas that staff have control over and not deal with issues that schools have minimal influence over, for example parents, government policy and pupil backgrounds. Such is the breadth of issues related to behaviour that it is inevitable that certain areas will be omitted and others understated.

3   **Professional development is important** The ideas and approaches suggested within the book have a theoretical base for which there is no apology as theory, research and effective practice interact to bring about professional development and substantive change in schools. It is hoped that staff in schools will undertake all or some of the tasks in order to arrive at their own personal answers.

4   **A sharing culture is essential** Central to the thinking behind the book is that behaviour management cannot be decontextualised from the school, its staff, culture, history, pedagogy, catchment area and all other individual forces that impact upon that school. Real change and effective behaviour policy is brought about best in a school climate and organisation where expertise is shared although, even in a school with a strong collaborative culture, it is often the case that effective practice is shared reluctantly. The extraction of the most suitable of the ideas explored and exercises offered in this book is essential and can form part of the

research that staff need to undertake into their practices as they seek, through enquiry, to enhance both their professional knowledge, understanding and practice and the behaviour policy of their school.

5   **It is important to develop a whole school policy** There is a belief that a whole school policy not only reflects staff practices but drives them. To facilitate the development of all aspects of the policy each chapter contains a series of questions, issues and challenges that lead to decisions that inform a whole school policy – inevitably a personal one, but hopefully one which can be adapted by the staff or school for their own needs.

Policy outlines, processes and principles

This chapter examines the nature of a behaviour management policy and advocates that it should inform positive relationships in schools. There are suggestions for ways in which it can be constructed, reviewed and evaluated. Emphasis is placed on the importance of a range of staff being involved, if not all staff, and the process of discussion and debate that needs to be engaged with before any final written version is published.

The issue of behaviour management in schools constantly comes to the forefront of the concerns of school professionals. Discussion and debate in various arenas, especially the media, fail to arrive at any kind of consensus, other than to suggest that it is serious and that the behaviour of young people, not only teenagers but also young children, is often deemed to be getting worse. The debate is often characterised by two sets of opinions which appear polarised. On the one hand, there are those for whom the only answer is sending children with behaviour difficulties to special schools or centres so that 'teachers can get on with their job', which is seen as delivering the curriculum. On the other hand, there are those who believe that teaching is about helping young people to change and mature to take their place in a highly complex society and that this is best achieved through countering the negative pressures that exist for children by providing inclusive environments and stable, positive classroom climates. There was a recent case in the UK of a media debate in which the two positions rehearsed their arguments with increasing heat and lack of respect for each other's positions. As the debate became ever more acrimonious the participants displayed the kinds of behaviours that all parties were bemoaning such as constant interruption, belittling others and presenting views in an aggressive manner. The debate crystallised around a single case study of a teenager who had sworn extensively at a member of staff. One solution was immediate exclusion and the reply was that, given fair and equal application of the rule, such a response, if applied universally, would lead to a sharp decline in student numbers and a massive special unit building programme! There was no resolution of the conflict and no solution arrived at and, although mention was made of the fact that schools are caught in traps from which there appear to be no release buttons, it did not foster a more understanding approach.

The motivation of a school to continue to work with pupils whose behaviour is difficult is often a mixture of the altruistic and pragmatic. In the case of the former it is a professional desire to keep working with the pupil and looking for ways to bring about change. In the case of the latter schools often need to keep pupils on their pupil register because their funding is linked to pupil numbers, therefore exclusion leads to funding decline. However, schools are also driven by a standards agenda and know that difficult behaviour can impact on learning and pupil achievement. They lose if they keep pupils and they lose if they do not, but most teachers and teaching assistants want to work with pupils with behaviour difficulties and seek to help them to change and achieve in schools. School often represents the best opportunity to break into what is perceived as a downward spiral. This positive attitude is encapsulated in a statement that sets out how the broad areas of pupil behaviour will be approached – the behaviour management policy. What follows is about that policy, its framework, the values that underpin it, its aims and the practice that it seeks to nurture or counter.

What is a behaviour policy?

At its simplest the function of a policy on behaviour, or indeed a policy on any aspect of a school, is to ensure that all interested parties know the ideas and practices that will underpin day-to-day life in the school. But a policy can be more than a document that mirrors practice; it can be a statement of aspirations and represent a direction that is forward and dynamic. It is here that *the message of respect and dignity emerges*. McNamara (1999) identifies three levels in the management of pupil behaviour. Level 1 is a pupil management policy, Level 2 looks at classroom practices and Level 3 at individual pupil management strategies. All three are covered in this book but, although separated as chapters, they link together and are part of a single coherent policy that permeates much that goes on in an effective school.

STAFF DEVELOPMENT EXERCISE

SDE 1.1 WHAT IS A BEHAVIOUR POLICY?

In small groups, answer questions a–c. Then, a whole group discussion, examine your own school's statement or seek to create one.

a Which statement below do you relate to most and why?

b Which statement is the best description of the behaviour policy in your school?

c Create your own description of a policy you would like to see in your school. Begin with: 'It is a policy that …'

1 It is a document that describes our practices and sets out clearly what is expected of pupils.

2 It is a document that states what kind of school this is, what rules are in place, what rewards we offer and what sanctions apply if rules are broken.

3 It is a document that represents the ideas and values that we hold to be true about our school, informs the standards of behaviour we expect and sets out aspirations for the development of positive relationships in our school.

A crucial word in the third statement is 'we'. 'We' may be the senior managers of the school, even *the* senior manager given the task of writing the document over a cold weekend prior to potential inspection, which is both cynical and regrettably has been known. 'We' could be staff who, after extensive discussion and deliberation, have reached agreement about their beliefs, hopes and practices. 'We' could also represent staff who, after extensive discussion with pupils, parents and governors, have reached consensus about best practices and aspirations. Whatever 'we' stands for, effective policy is linked to collaborative approaches, shared school based research and a recognition of the value of the process of devising policy and not about imposed solutions, instant fixes and simple prescriptions for success. If the argument against this is 'we do not have the time to develop policy in this way', consideration might be given to the time lost through ineffective approaches, disagreement and demoralisation of staff, dealing with parental problems and stress related illness in staff. The value of the journey cannot be emphasised enough.

Writing a policy never really starts with a blank piece of paper because much is already decided, if not made explicit. The experience and values of the authors of the document, the framework that they are working within such as any previous documents, the school structure and the requirements of external inspection and internal governor groups all contribute to the starting point. One possible starting point would be to gather data from a variety of parties including governors, parents, other schools, all staff and, of course, pupils. In terms of application of policy it might circumvent future problems if the policy is endorsed by parents or their representative groups, or, even better than endorsement, if parent groups feel that they have made a contribution to the construction phase. In seeking parental opinions the school not only receives their views but is also able to raise awareness about key issues and generate a two-way flow of information. When confronted by disagreements later in the school year from individual parents, to have the support of general parental opinion helps counter potential conflict.

Before moving on to consider the structure and range of policies one key theme needs to be elaborated on – consistency. Throughout this book the significance of consistency is emphasised. This means that the application of policy and the procedures developed through it should be the same for all. It is the promotion of a view that pupils believe in fairness and wish to see it applied by and modelled by staff. However, it does not mean that teachers and teaching assistants respond robotically and chant the mantras of policy metronomically. Staff bring variety of personality and professional skills to the classroom and pupils sense this. In the case of personality, a sense of humour, perhaps eccentricity or passion for subject, can all be attractive for pupils and the plea for consistency herein does not inhibit any of these. In terms of temperament, everyone has off days, including pupils, and relationships in classrooms are the better for them as this reflects social norms. The consistency referred to here is about processes, ideas and mutual support. Individuality is essential as long as it does not undermine the work of colleagues.

Contemporary thinking, advice and legislation often lead to a formula for a policy that results in statements of values and expectations which are linked, rules and sanctions for breaking rules, the rights and responsibilities embodied within them and how they influence relationships. Often included are the procedures that support practice, and show how the policy was devised and what action is required should it be deemed necessary. Procedural statements help pupils, staff and parents understand what to do, who to contact and who is responsible for particular aspects. Sometimes a policy is designed around or makes reference to specific theories that influence or support practices. In this case, compatibility of theories is essential in order that ways of dealing with seemingly contradictory approaches do not have to be developed (Porter, 2000).

A comprehensive behaviour policy will have statements that include most of, if not all, the following:

- the mission of the school and how the behaviour policy relates to that mission

- ethos, values, guiding principles, expectations of standards and beliefs of staff, all of which are different, and the selection will match other policies and staff choices (these will cross over into all aspects of school life and therefore all policies)

- theories, thinking and ideas that have influenced policy and behaviour management practices (these may have crossed over into other aspects of school life and therefore other policies) – the staff version of the policy may have an additional set of skills that are effective and relate to acknowledged theories

- rights that are championed and preserved and responsibilities that secure those rights

- rewards given for positive behaviour

- rules that have been agreed and which relate to all the above

- sanctions, punishments or consequences that will be imposed if rules are broken and rights not preserved

- procedures that need to be followed, especially during non-contact times such as lunchtime

- contacts, support and procedures that help in explaining and enforcing policy and practice for parents and carers

- evaluation, review and research processes.

STAFF DEVELOPMENT EXERCISE
SDE 1.2 THE POLICY FRAMEWORK

In smalls groups consider your responses to the questions a–c and then convene as a staff or larger group to share views.

a What are the strengths and weaknesses of your policy when it is examined against the list below?

b Would you make any changes, additions or deletions to the list?

c How might the school go about addressing the issues raised, for example through working groups, school councils, external expertise?

1 the mission of the school and how the behaviour policy relates to that mission

2 ethos, values, guiding principles, beliefs of staff, expectations of standards

3 theories, thinking and ideas

4 effective skills in preventing and managing disruption (staff version only perhaps)

5 rights and responsibilities

6 rewards given for positive behaviour

7 rules that have been agreed

8 sanctions, punishments or consequences

9 contacts, support and procedures that help in explaining and enforcing policy and practice for parents and carers

10 evaluation, review and research processes

All too often, after a few idealistic words about ethos, values and aims, the main elements of a policy are sanctions and rewards that focus on the negative behaviours of a few and not the positive or neutral behaviours of the many. Most of the document is taken up with defining negative behaviours and what will happen if pupils transgress. It creates an impression of focusing on negative, authoritarian approaches and, in some cases, reactive or crisis management. In addition, it is counterproductive to make initial statements that are altruistic and full of aspirations but are then followed by only sanction or punishment based information. To address this, some schools approach behaviour policy from the opposite side which starts with a positive relations policy that considers the school's vision for supporting the development of relationships within the school and beyond it including relationships in the future. Such a policy will also look at the expectations that the school has for its pupils in both learning and behaviour, which is a false divide that often is reflected in schools systems. Behaviour policy is about learning and good classroom management and vice versa.

One element not mentioned above which might be added to the policy is how it addresses contemporary requirements in terms of skills. Fortunately there has been a movement away from 'competences' as the way in which knowledge, skills and attributes of education staff are defined. At one level, it can be helpful in that it deconstructs professional elements into specific defined areas. It helps to itemise what is required and makes clear to teacher and teaching assistant organisations what they need to provide and nurture in their pupils. However, it is a term that conveys a form of regression to the mean in that it says, 'if you are okay or average at this then that's fine'. Application of this thinking to behaviour management skills limits potential. What if you are *not* satisfied with being 'competent' or 'okay' or 'average' and being competent does not adequately describe your personal or professional knowledge, skills and attributes? What if nothing but excellent or outstanding will be good enough for your aspirations, as an individual or as a school, for working with your pupils? Now the term used appears to be 'standards' and it is significant how many directly refer to behaviour and its management. The following, all addressed in this book, are from the Professional Standards for Higher Level Teaching Assistants and are likely to have implications for a rigorous behaviour management policy.

1.3   They demonstrate and promote the positive values, attitudes and behaviour they expect from the pupils with whom they work.

2.9   They know a range of strategies to establish a purposeful learning environment and to promote good behaviour.

3.1.2 Working within a framework set by the teacher, they plan their role in lessons including how they will provide feedback to pupils and colleagues on pupils' learning and behaviour.

3.3.4 They use behaviour management strategies, in line with the school's policy and procedures, which contribute to a purposeful learning environment.

The stages of policy construction

Individual schools will establish their own ways of discussing, debating and developing a behaviour policy, which is not an easy or short process. Once completed it requires review and recapitulation and if found to be successful, it may not need major modifications. Time spent on the early stages will pay off later. What is advocated below may seem long-winded but a speedily cobbled together alternative over a weekend by a member of senior management has little chance of success. The following joke on the subject contains many truths.

> The degree of effectiveness of a policy or specific approach is inversely proportional to the level of management that devised it. In the end it was like mating elephants in that:

- it was done at a very high level

- it involved a great deal of bellowing and screaming

- it took two years to get results

- and we were crushed by the results!

Table 1.1 is a suggested outline and works on the principle of extensive staff involvement at all levels of decision making. It requires four stages – planning, first day, second day and distribution – and includes several staff sessions. The first stage is likely to last about a day and is obviously suited to a non-pupil day, and the second about half a day. In between the meetings there are things to be decided and written. The Staff Development Exercises in this book will help with many of those tasks depending on the school's approach. It is crucial to choose someone to co-ordinate activities and function as the facilitator for any SDEs and resulting decisions.

Table 1.1 *The stages of policy construction*

Stage	Additional information
Stage 1: Planning and Preparation	
Choose the co-ordinator(s)	It does not have to be one person and they do not have to be senior managers, but an individual or a small group will need to be the 'change drivers'. They will co-ordinate all meetings. A group may also function as the review group (see Table 1.2).
Gather data	Perceptions of staff, parents, pupils and governors may be sought on key issues, for example their views on sanctions and rewards.
Decide on main headings	Although not set in stone, they function as the main agenda.
Plan first staff meeting	Agree a time for a long meeting, perhaps a professional development day. Set the agenda – the greater the preparation the more likely it is that decisions will be reached. Agree who will attend beyond the staff (depending on what 'staff' means).
Stage 2: First Staff Meeting	
Phase 1	1 Set out aims of the day. 2 Present summary of findings from the preparatory research. 3 Discuss and agree broad principles and mission statements (samples may help).
Phase 2	Sub-groups work on ideas for practical elements, for example rules, rewards, sanctions, consequences and contact procedures. Appropriate SDEs can support their deliberations.
Phase 3	Set up writing group tasks and agree time for first draft. Agree consultation groups, for example for first draft governors, pupils.
Interim	Writing group works on draft policy statement.
Stage 3: Second Staff Meeting	
Phase 1	All staff discuss initial aspects of the first draft.
Phase 2	Sub-groups meet again to agree modifications if required.
Phase 3	All staff make final recommendations including deadline, distribution and review dates.
Stage 4: Presentation and Distribution	
Final draft	Produced by policy writer(s) and presented to relevant parties, for example governors, parent teacher association. Finally, it needs to be ratified by governors, which will be easy as they have been informed or involved throughout.

In education, as in some other professions, we are used to policy construction being a process of writing a summary of beliefs, aspirations and practice and placing the result in a file. This process has a dual role. First, it represents the aspirations and values of the staff and shows how they are handling key issues such equal opportunities, access to the curriculum, etc. Secondly, it provides a buffer in a world in which schools are subject to extensive inspection regimes that demand a framework of policies to be in place and, also, an increasingly litigious world in which legal requirements sometimes take precedence over professional practice and principle. Such are the pressures on modern schools to conform to the needs of outside agencies that their own identity may not fully emerge through their policy statements. As a practice, generating policy documents solely through pressures from external forces devalues the whole process and undermines the final product, both as a document and the practices it aims to inform and as a professional statement.

Balancing the positive and negative aspects of behaviour policy is not easy. Often, in devising policy, schools resort to narrow sanction based statements that tell pupils what happens when rules are broken and rights infringed. In contrast, other schools seek to emphasise what positive behaviours are and how they are endorsed and rewarded. Such emphasis on the positive is linked to a desire to improve the self-esteem of pupils and is predicated on the idea that increased self-esteem is an aspiration of schools and an inspiration to learning.

Table 1.2 is designed to support the process of the creation of the policy by addressing key issues that secure a rigorous engagement with what will be significant areas. It also includes the beginning of the evaluative process. It is not comprehensive and further sections can be added, but it highlights key questions that review groups would consider as they monitor successes, celebrations and concerns.

Table 1.2 *Evaluating, reviewing and researching the behaviour policy*

Issues and questions	Possible solutions
Examination and review How will the policy be monitored to secure the success of your deliberations?	Review group to undertake a short meeting every term and make suggestions where necessary. This process is repeated each term and different staff are included.
Representativeness Does it represent the values, attitudes and practices of the school and the wider community?	Two staff from the review group plus headteacher, parent or governor to undertake a short review meeting on this specific issue and make suggestions if necessary.
Flexibility How will it incorporate the values, stances and good practices of all staff?	There is a myth that 'you've either got it or you haven't got it' (Olsen and Cooper, 2001) when it comes to managing disruption. In reality all staff possess the potential for good ideas and practices and these need to be translated into the review process. Staff are invited to list their positive attributes in behaviour management and their recent successes.
Involvement and ownership Will it involve all parties, including staff and parents? (The DfES (2004) Key Stage 3 behaviour and attendance strategy emphasises their significance in successful policy construction.)	Any review of policy and practice might have the views of pupils and parents represented and this may be formal or informal. Parents' workshops that provide opportunities to debate and discuss are preferable to those that tell them what you have decided.
Pupil participation Do all parties agree on the: ■ definitions of disruption, rudeness, bullying, etc.? ■ policy expectations are realistic for all pupils? ■ viability of the rewards and sanctions components?	Staff and pupils discuss key terminology and agree definitions where appropriate. Pupils discuss or are informed of expectations, rewards and consequences of misbehaviour. Feedback is presented to the review group.
Resources and professional development ■ Will the policy require staff to embrace new skills and training? ■ Will the policy be enhanced by research into its effectiveness and perceptions of various groups about it?	Central to a dynamic policy is securing increased skill levels and the need for professional development at all levels will mean working closely with those staff responsible for professional development. Any staff working towards further or higher education qualifications might be encouraged to research one aspect of the policy and the practices that arise from it as part of their studies. Perceptions of involved parties can reveal useful and relevant information.
Consultation beyond Is the policy simply a reaction to the requirement to generate it or does it seek to examine opportunities for good practice from both outside and within the school?	Good practice can be shared through links with other schools and agencies. Many schools construct their policy in isolation as a mirror of their particular culture and opportunities to share and inform each other are rare. The value of shared professional development cannot be overstated when looking not only at common practices but also the therapeutic value of sharing problems.

What to include and what to leave out

The scope and range of a policy is a key issue and decisions will need to be reached on a variety of issues such as attendance, now included within the DfES (2004) Key Stage 3 Strategy in England and Wales, pastoral issues, inclusion and bullying. Bullying is rarely a matter of focus for the behaviour policy and there may be good reasons for this. However, Chaplain (2003: 83) emphasises how behaviour policy can contribute towards a school's overall climate. This is essential as it should not be dislocated in thinking and practice from other policies as it not only contributes to differing policy areas such as bullying but can reflect the effective practice determined within them. A behaviour policy should never be seen in isolation, but as an integral part of how a school perceives itself and wishes to be seen by others and a key element of this is likely to be relationships. Therefore, it is perhaps surprising that schools elect to have separate anti-bullying and behaviour policies despite the common threads that are likely to be found in both policies. Possible reasons for this are diverse.

- The inspection body for schools, Ofsted, encourages schools to have anti-bullying policy statements and this implies separation from other policies.

- The academic and professional development communities have elected to research and write about bullying as if it exists outside the range of other behaviours found in schools.

- Bullying policies have as their focus negative pupil–pupil relationships and do not usually consider other relationships such as staff–pupil, which assumes a narrow interpretation of bullying.

The meaning of the term 'bullying' varies (Lee, 2006) and is in a constant state of flux, currently through the practice of 'cyberbullying', for example the use of texting and computers as media to hurt and intimidate others. Given a broader view of the term it can be seen as a crucial contributor towards the development of a behaviour policy, if not an integral part of it. The decision that a school makes is whether what appears to be relationship problems should come under its behaviour policies that are all too often narrowly tied to classroom management and staff–pupil relationships. Behaviour policies are about relationship matters – relationships with peers, adults and the classroom itself – and bullying is about learning as few pupils who are being picked on feel safe in school and this impedes their learning.

Table 1.3 illustrates that negative behaviours are not just the domain of the pupils and deliberations for the policy might also include how staff wish to relate to pupils and to each other. The impact of adult role models on pupil relationships cannot be overstated. It follows naturally that any comprehensive systemic approach should involve all areas in that system as well as all its participants and there is no doubt that policy statements about the nature of supportive and professional relationships will be a richer document.

Table 1.3 *Bullying: a broad look at relationships in school*

Pupil–pupil bullying: the assertion of negative power over other individuals or groups through intent to cause hurt. It may be a single act or a 'bullying relationship' that is repeated and is carried out over a period of time.

Examples
- Threats and intimidation to extract money
- Exclusion from social groups
- Violent acts against those who cannot defend themselves
- Hurtful texting

Staff–pupil bullying: the assertion of negative power over individual, groups or classes through belittling or aggressive behaviour. Pupils feel upset and resentful, self-esteem is damaged and the learning experience is negative.

Examples
- Personally addressed sarcasm and put-downs
- Derogatory hurtful comments
- Unjust threats to use power to blame and punish
- Deliberate exclusion of pupil in need of support

Pupil–staff bullying: the assertion of negative power by a pupil or group of pupils through causing staff to feel threatened, intimidated or undermined. It is deliberate, hurtful and causes stress.

Examples
- Name calling and other forms of verbal intimidation
- Negative comments about race or sexuality
- Deliberate group action to disrupt lessons
- Unfounded threats to 'tell' parents

Staff–staff bullying: the assertion of negative power through belittling or aggressive behaviour that aims to undermine the professionalism of a member of staff. It can be an individual act or a persistent feature of the relationship.

Examples
- Derision of staff involvement in professional development
- Overuse of hierarchical position to threaten action
- Staffroom derision of innovation
- Denial of promotion for personal reasons

Defining misbehaviour

As with defining bullying, attempts to define misbehaviour or troublesome behaviour are fraught with problems for policy devising processes. The problems of attempting to remove subjectivity have been highlighted in the literature (McManus, 1995). They are threefold.

1   If misbehaviour is defined by placing emphasis on the individual pupil in the classroom *interrupting the teaching process, it is too narrow* and many pupils requiring additional support or making significant observations could be seen as 'troublesome' as they interrupt what is going on in the classroom. In addition, regarding the school as a system means that all that exists within the influence of the school is significant and troublesome behaviour occurs in many environments beyond the classroom.

2   If there is *no consideration of specific factors* then generalised definitions of troublesome behaviour *make no allowances for context*. Definitions of troublesome behaviour are likely to vary considerably between a special school for pupils on the autistic spectrum, an early years setting and a large secondary school.

3   Attempts to define misbehaviour are *problematic and subjective* as what one person sees as significant misbehaviour, others might consider as 'trying it on'. It has been defined as 'behaviour which seriously interferes with the teaching process and/or seriously upsets the normal running of the school' (Lawrence et al., 1984). The emphasis on *serious* interference invites staff to begin to define what is *serious* in their school and therefore renders the definition context specific and subjective – which may not be such a bad thing!

Definitions of disruptive or troublesome behaviour have limitations in written policies in that they place boundaries around what is and what is not acceptable which, at first glance, is desirable. However, these boundaries may change over time or be incomplete. One way to overcome this is through lists of prohibited behaviours, commonly found in policies, which are useful as illustrations and guidelines for staff, although they also serve to tell some pupils what to do to get into trouble – which may be helpful for them! Any attempt to define behaviours for younger pupils certainly demands illustrative examples and invites opportunities to discuss the reasoning behind them which, in turn, looks to the rules (Chapter 3).

A questionnaire that formed part of a professional development session that I undertook with 36 teaching assistants from a single secondary school suggests that understanding of what misbehaviour is has common features across the primary and secondary divide and across the two key classroom roles of teachers and teaching assistants. In keeping with research into teachers' views in primary schools (Merrett and Wheldall, 1984) the most common responses to behaviours that they found *difficult to stop* were low level classroom disorders (43 per cent) such as 'talking out of turn', 'low key misbehaviour', 'ignoring requests', 'shouting out' and 'bad' or 'abusive language' (25 per cent). 'Rudeness' (25 per cent) and 'bad language' (14 per cent) were the most consistent responses when asked in the questionnaire what induced their *anger*. However, when asked about what they saw as *senseless* no single behaviour emerged but they did step beyond pupils' behaviours and saw pedagogical matters as significant. While the majority focused on pupils' behaviours such as 'damage to property', others began to see the problems defined in policy issues such as 'if a behaviour policy is not followed up' and 'inconsistency with rules relating to jewellery/make up/uniform'. If wearing jewellery falls within a school's definition of inappropriate or troublesome behaviour, some form of consistency from all staff in its application would seem to be essential or it becomes pointless to list it. Wearing jewellery and not wearing school uniform are threats to the image a school wishes to portray and perhaps its ethos, but they are not interruptions to learning or direct threats to the safety of others. Yet all too often they become bundled into a list that makes no distinction and therefore does not help young people to see the consequence of their actions.

Your current school system

Constructing school based behaviour policies raises fundamental questions about the nature of the school, its culture and the processes that rest content within it. As stated above, it also raises questions about the policy generation process and what exactly a policy is. Mention has already been made of the model in which it can be divided into short statements of the rights of members of the school, both staff and pupils, followed by a consideration of what happens when these rights are threatened or violated. Where schools have stepped beyond these statements there tends to be further reflection on intricate questions about the school and the ways that it addresses them. The three questions in SDE 1.3, which are a starting point, can be a risk in a organisation that lacks confidence but are a trigger for discussion in one that is self-assured. They help by beginning the process of evaluation of the system in which the pupils operate.

STAFF DEVELOPMENT EXERCISE

SDE 1.3 EVALUATION OF THE CURRENT SYSTEM

a As an individual or in small groups, consider questions 1–3 and supply a maximum of three answers for each one.

b Share the findings in larger groups and come to some form of consensus, then for question 1 discuss how the agreed components can be extended and enhanced. For questions 2 and 3 consider one short-term and one long-term action that will help – if you think more could and should be done then note those items.

c Decide what changes will need to be made to the current behaviour policy and any other policies to embrace the areas identified.

1 What does this school do to prevent misbehaviour?

(a) ....

(b) ....

(c) ....

2 What about this school permits or licences misbehaviour?

(a) ....

(b) ....

(c) ....

3 What about this school even promotes misbehaviour?

(a) ....

(b) ....

(c) ....

Mission statements and beyond

Walk into a school where teachers are locked in to a 'them and us' mindset, where students are seen as either good or bad … and you'll find a school in which children are disengaged, underachieving and resentful.

(Klein, 1999: xvii)

At the outset of any behaviour policy there need to be statements of principles that inform what follows. Any rules, reward and sanction system developed by schools and expressed in their policy is probably one of the most tangible expressions of the values they hold dear and of how those values and a mission statement that enshrines them are translated into the school's system. It may well be that the mission statement will head up the policy document and relate strongly, if not be identical, to the school's general mission statement. Inevitably there will be general statements which, nonetheless, set the tone for what follows and need to be considered by all. It is in this early discussion that the:

■ process of sharing ideas is set

■ opportunity for the policy to be representative of all staff and, if deemed appropriate, student groups is determined and ownership established

■ principles are finalised after discussion and debate

■ links between broader principles and detailed practices are made clearer

■ review processes can be instituted.

If it is more the Principal behind the policy than the principles, in other words it is a statement of the aspirations of the headteacher and key management staff, then staff have no feeling of ownership. If the principles of relationships, climate and discipline are formulated by people other than those who enforce and abide by them then dislocation is the outcome. Alternatively, if there is a process of high involvement then high levels of understanding, reflection and responsibility ensue. Similarly, if there is no process of review then the policy is static, but if reviewed by a range of involved staff and students, affirmations of success, adjustments and major changes take place.

In many ways much of what will be decided will be linked to how staff perceive their own professionalism and capacity to make change and maybe, at a basic level, to how they perceive children. Jenks (1996) talks about two seemingly competitive images in thinking about children. The first, Apollonian, perceives children as innocents, inherently good and angelic, who become corrupted by adults in the process of growing up. The second, Dionysian, views children as inherently naughty, impish and in need of discipline so that they can be socialised into the adult world. Whatever images adults in school have of their pupils is likely to influence both policy and practice in dealing with disruptive and problematic behaviour.

17

STAFF DEVELOPMENT EXERCISE

SDE 1.4 MAJOR STATEMENTS

In groups or as individuals, consider statements 1–4 and then answer questions a–c.

a Which of the statements would you see as most appropriate for your own setting?

b What adaptations would you make to the statement you chose in a)?

c What are the implications for the practice of behaviour management in each of the statements?

1 We aim to maintain a disciplined and friendly atmosphere within which everyone in the school treats each other with courtesy, respect and tolerance.

2 We believe in the importance of encouraging pupils to behave in a caring, co-operative and self-disciplined manner.

3 Pupils are expected to develop a sense of right and wrong.

4 Our aim is to ensure that the rights and responsibilities of those at the school are protected and upheld and that the buildings are well cared for by all users.

STAFF DEVELOPMENT EXERCISE
SDE 1.5 INDICATORS OF THE SCHOOL ETHOS

In small groups, answer questions a–d before reconvening as a staff or in larger groups to compare findings and consider the implications.

a Undertake the scaling task below by ranking your school on a 1–10 scale for each criteria (1 being low).

b How do you know what the strengths are (how are they demonstrated in school)?

c How do you know what the weaknesses are (how are they demonstrated in school)?

d Determine what needs to be done to secure higher numbers in areas seen as weak or less strong and how it will be done. (It may be better to think about turning a score of 5 into 7 rather than changing a 3 into a 10. After all, if a situation has persisted for a long time there may be fundamental reasons that will take a long time to overhaul.)

e What would you change or add to the list?

Ethos indicators	The degree to which …	Scale 1–10
Pupil morale	pupils enjoy school and find it safe and satisfying.	
Staff morale	staff feel that they receive support and recognition from colleagues, senior management and parents.	
Staff job satisfaction	staff value their professional role and feel that they are doing a worthwhile job.	
Physical environment	the school is seen as a safe, comfortable and pleasant environment for work and leisure.	
Learning context	classrooms are seen as stimulating environments.	
Staff–pupil relationships	harmonious relations exist between staff and pupils and they treat one another with courtesy and respect.	
Equality and justice	there are policies agreed on and understood by staff and reflected in their day-to-day practice.	
Extra-curricular activities	opportunities are provided for learning and social activity outside the classrooms and seen as enjoyable and beneficial by pupils and staff.	
School leadership	there is inspiration, direction and support provided by the headteacher and senior management team.	
Discipline	the school provides an ordered environment in which staff feel able to carry out their duties and pupils feel able to work without interruption and intimidation.	
Information to parents	parents feel that they are kept informed about their children's progress and developments in the school.	
Parent–staff consultation	parents and staff have opportunities to share their expertise and feel that it has been of benefit to pupils, parents and other staff.	

A major feature of the opening statement of any school policy will be an attempt to define the ethos of the school. Ethos is a vague term which, if developed in school policies, is likely to appear in general statements about the school but when unpackaged as a concept, most components have implications for, if not direct statements about, the behaviour management element. The Scottish Office [SOED] (1992) produced a series of indicators of what it considered the ethos of a school and all have implications for pupil (and staff) feelings and behaviour. SDE 1.5 is an adapted version. It will be worth looking at the indicators and considering in what ways the behaviour of pupils will impact upon them.

Although it could be constructed in others ways the list of criteria highlight the centrality of behaviour management to how a school appears and the messages, both hidden and open, that it gives off. The physical environment can covey messages about the school and how it is cared for but it can also have a more direct impact on behaviour. Sharp and Smith (1994) noticed positive changes in playground behaviour that resulted from redesigning playgrounds as part of the Sheffield project and how significant environment can be in influencing positive behaviour. Sometimes the ethos is almost intangible, hard to locate, even ethereal, yet somehow so evident from earliest entry into a school and it is sometimes better defined as 'atmosphere'. A positive ethos may be hard to define but you know it when you meet it. Nonetheless the SOED criteria provide a useful beginning for the self-analysis process and some of the less obvious elements connect to improvement in behaviour. Ultimately the statement of ethos will be a reflection of the school, how the school wishes to be seen and the direction in which it sees itself moving. Statements may be ambitious and creative, for as Cornwall suggests (2004), schools have been fundamentally authoritarian by structure, if not by nature, since the 1800s but now they are beginning to redefine themselves and not only *reflect* new patterns of learning and new notions of behaviour in society but *drive them* forward.

At the end of this chapter you will have decided:

■ the personnel who will create or review the behaviour policy

■ the degree to which all staff will be involved in or consulted about policy generation

■ the breadth of the remit of the policy

■ the structure of the policy

■ the process that will be adopted for its construction

■ the key issues about current practice and aspirations that need to be considered.

Theory that guides policy and practice

2

This chapter considers the importance of theory and the ideas that underpin theories for behaviour management practice. A brief summary of the main theoretical approaches and their links to how much power they give to pupils and adults in the classroom is followed by a closer exploration of the systemic approach, which has specific implications for creators of policy in behaviour management.

The importance of theory

Behaviour management is no different from any other area of education in that it has key thinkers and theorists who have contributed to debate, discussion and the building of a body of work that informs practice. Many theories explicitly and directly inform school practice although many are put into practice by staff in schools without high levels of knowledge about the theory behind them. Some schools appear to have a negative view of theory while others embrace it as they would do any idea that enhances practice.

A colleague was working in a school on a professional development day. While introducing him his host said, 'Now Charlie you are not going to give us any of that theory, are you? We want solutions, practical ideas and things that work'. If only behaviour management (and most other aspects of education) were that simple. Indeed fortunes have been made by some who say that they have effortless and straightforward solutions to educational problems – just witness the plethora of recent initiatives and still the search for answers continues. My colleague knew that any quest for simple or complete remedies was futile (DES, 1989). His response was to emphasise that he would be making practical suggestions but that he could not divorce those suggestions from the theory behind them because it helped everyone to understand why they were likely to work and what other practices were related to any given theory. So rightly there was some theory and no apology for it and the same applies here!

Theory is essential because it:

- is an *expectation of professionals* that they possess knowledge, deep understanding and ideas about their work context (school and classroom)

- can be examined to see if the values and practices that underpin a theory *harmonise with the values and practices of the school*, classroom or member of staff

- provides a context in which practices are understood, helps to *explain why things work* and highlights similar ideas and practices that might also work

- *creates a vocabulary* that aids understanding

- invites *consideration of similar ideas, alternatives and thinking 'otherwise'*.

Most of the ideas included later in this book and in other texts relate to specific schools of thought that have been developed. Some texts, which may be written by the creator of the approach, outline its principles and methods. Other texts analyse and summarise a range of theories about behavioural approaches (Ayers and Gray, 1998; Porter, 2000; Wolfgang, 2005). Ways of categorising and comparing theories have also been developed. In recent years there has been a considerable interest in Assertive Discipline (Canter and Canter, 2001) and schools were encouraged to integrate it into their practices. However, imposed, quick fix solutions are unlikely to work unless staff are skilled in them and, even more significantly, understand, agree with and consistently apply the ideas that underpin them. 'Off the shelf' behaviour management theories have little chance of success unless the theory resonates with staff values, practices, expertise and the school culture – and even then success will be limited because, as suggested below, eclecticism of approaches is likely to be required.

Porter (2000) citing Young (1992) describes how theory can translate into practice in eclectic ways which can also be fraught with dangers. First, there is, *synthetic eclecticism*, which is the integration of compatible theories to form something which can end up being more complex than any of the original theories. Of the three forms of eclecticism it is this one that she recommends because, given compatibility of the common features and providing that the hybrid does not contain contradictions, it permits a personalisation of the theories and may lead to more commitment than incorporating the ideas of someone else. One theme that resonates throughout the literature on implementation of the major ideas is that staff need to adapt effective practices to best match the needs of their pupils, their teaching strengths and the available resources (Tankersley et al., 2004). Secondly, there is *technical eclecticism* which draws upon one main theory and borrows some approaches from others. This assumes that there is compatibility in the underlying theories which, if not the case, will lead to practices that are contradictory. Finally, *atheoretical eclecticism* lacks a theoretical base and therefore methods which appear suitable for the immediate situation are applied. This lack of a rationale means that it is 'not an option for professionals' (Porter, 2000: 13) and is too undisciplined.

Schools of intervention

It is not an ambition of this book to consider all the main theories of behaviour management in any depth, although some will be mentioned in greater detail later, but it is intended to advise on the application of and links between theory and intervention approaches to policy and practice in schools. However, there will be examples from some theories which are offered as ways of thinking about the link between theory and practice and how staff might address policy construction that has a theoretical underpinning.

Olsen and Cooper (2001) describe three schools of interventions – behavioural, cognitive and systemic – each of which has drawbacks and limitations. However, they advocate that the most effective interventions for pupils with behavioural difficulties will draw upon all three schools and that models should be combined. They maintain that the portrayal of theories being in conflict with one another as unhelpful and reliance on single approaches militates against any form of the synthetic eclecticism mentioned above. Not every perspective fits the needs of the pupil, the skills of the staff or the culture of the school and it is all too easy to fall into the trap of believing that lack of progress as a result of one approach means that there has been deterioration in a pupil's behaviour and the pupil is beyond hope. What may be required is for staff to consider the validity of the intervention. It is possible that they have been using the wrong approach, or using the right approach incorrectly.

One way of categorising theories is to focus on **perspectives of interventions**, in other words how staff as individuals and schools as institutions respond. Olsen and Cooper's (2001) three categories are:

■ behaviourist perspectives

■ cognitive approaches

■ systemic approaches.

Both Visser (2000) and Barrow (1998) add:

■ psychodynamic perspectives.

Barrow (1998) advocates one further category:

■ transactional analysis.

Behaviourist perspectives

Behaviourism is the approach in most common usage in schools and looks at behaviour as a learned response to stimuli. Behaviour problems are caused either by pupils responding wrongly to stimuli or by deficient stimuli inducing inappropriate behaviour. Its central tenet is that the best way to help pupils who exhibit problem behaviours is *to teach the pupil new behaviours*. This is done by programmes which look at defining appropriate behaviour through rules and reinforcement through rewards and punishment, or sanctions in the case of troublesome behaviour. Assessment focuses on the specific observable behaviours of the pupil using behaviour checklists and observations (Ayers and Gray, 1998).

Cognitive approaches

The cognitive approaches emphasise that the best way to help pupils who exhibit problem behaviours is to *change the pupils' perceptions*. They are based on humane principles associated with counselling and through problem solving aim to promote empathy and understanding of maximising potential, and it is assumed that behaviour can be directly linked to cognitive processes. These approaches are manifested in schools through contracts that set targets and through discussion of incidents which help pupils to understand the position and feelings of others and involve changing pupils' beliefs, perceptions and thoughts about events. Pupils are encouraged to keep accounts of events and report on events as a means of providing information about why certain behaviours occurred. Assessment focuses on pupils' attitudes and beliefs in relation to peers, learning, teachers and school generally and can be undertaken through interviews and questionnaires.

Systemic approaches

The systemic approach, which is sometimes called the ecosystemic approach, is based upon the idea that the best way to help pupils who exhibit problem behaviours is *to focus on interactions*, in other words the connection of pupils and the people in their world – in a school's case the link with staff, classmates and peer groups, and outside the school the link with parents, carers and siblings. It also works on the premise that all behaviour has meaning or is serving a purpose for that individual even though it might be destructive. Change here involves staff analysing their responses and changing the way they respond in order to shift the relationship between the pupil and their behaviour. The pupil may not learn any new skills but the system in which they exist may interpret matters and respond differently. It involves changing expectations, seeing the situation differently (reframing) and seeking information from other staff (sleuthing). Assessment focuses on interactions between staff and pupils and perceptions of classroom and school interactions. Given that the focus here steps beyond the pupil and looks at the context, this approach needs greater consideration from a behaviour policy perspective and is explored in more depth later in the chapter.

Psychodynamic perspectives

Psychodynamic perspectives are based upon the idea that *how pupils feel about themselves* will influence, if not determine, their behaviour. It is based upon the notion that conscious behaviour is influenced by the unconscious mind which generates conflict within the child who is not aware of it or lacks insights into the conflict. A young child who experiences betrayal and rejection from adults outside school may find placing trust in them difficult in school and this manifests itself in defiance or anger. The specialised nature of this approach means its manifestation in the classroom has been limited. However, linked to this approach and of interest for staff in schools is the concept of a pupil's self-esteem and its relationship with achievement and behaviour. Particularly in early years settings, staff often incorporate opportunities to make sense of the world as pupils join the formal education system. The more extensive use of circle time allows pupils to share feelings, feel valued, value others and enjoy feedback that may enhance self-esteem.

Transactional analysis

In the case of transactional analysis the *focus is on the transactions taking place in corridors and classrooms and how staff and pupils react*. Each individual, no matter what age, functions in one of three 'ego-states' – adult, child or parent (Barrow et al., 2001). These states are not given and the individual has a choice about their ego-state but pupils, especially younger pupils, have little experience of making such choices so more responsibility rests with the adult in school based transactions. The person in child state may react in compliant or rebellious mode, while the person in parent state can be nurturing or overcontrolling. How often are pupil–staff transactions characterised by the pupil acting in rebellious mode and the member of staff functioning in an overcontrolling parent state with the incvitable emotional escalation into conflict and anger until breaking points are reached? The solution is to move ego states but the pupil may have little opportunity or experience of doing so, therefore staff find themselves with important choices about their own ego state.

The third state – adult – is the preferred option. It embodies the intellectual and rational state which is the choice for all parties to adopt but is usually easier for the member of staff. The alternative is the heated, stressful exchange which no one wins except perhaps onlookers who derive entertainment from the experience. However hard it is, staff are invariably more experienced at operating in adult mode and it is important that they retain that and encourage it in the pupil for whom it may be a long journey and one which they have no experience of, especially if life at home is dominated by overcontrolling parenting. So much effective conflict management is about redefining the problem, whether we respond personally or professionally, and securing a winning situation for all parties.

The power continuum

The different categories of theory are based upon their key ways of interpreting behaviour and developing a coherent and distinctive approach to practices in schools. Another method of categorising and contextualising theories examines intervention approaches and their relationship with the notion of teacher power in the form of a continuum with pupils possessing more power at one end and teachers being a more dominant force at the other. Wolfgang (2005) used the teacher's power continuum to construct three main groups that are outside the legalistic–coercive element imposed by the most extreme of behaviours and in which teachers and other staff have little choice, and also what he calls the 'proactive models' such as peer mediation which work with ideas that help to create school climates.

■ **Relationship/Listening:** these ideas and approaches focus on the therapeutic nature of managing classroom difficulties in which teachers emphasise the listening and relationship building element. An example of this is Harris's (1969) *I'm OK – you're OK* and the influence of transactional analysis is evident here.

■ **Confronting and Contracting:** these ideas and approaches integrate elements of the counselling approaches and contracting with pupils. Pupils are given the opportunity to make choices and understand the decisions they make and the consequences of those decisions. The works of William Glasser (1969, 1992) and Rudolf Dreikurs and colleagues (1990, 1998) are pivotal to this group of theorists.

■ Finally, there are those ideas which aim to be more controlling in the classroom and school through a framework of rules, rewards and punishments. Contemporary writers in this area include the Canters (2001) with their 'Assertive Discipline'. Wolfgang (2005) calls this group '**Rules and Consequences**' but consequences, of the 'natural' and 'logical' variety, are often more associated with Dreikurs. This point emphasises the dilemmas faced by those who categorise and seek to create 'watertight frameworks'. The emphasis on the third group is on bringing a sense of control through rewards and sanctions but even issues such as these are vulnerable to the question of who determines the rules and the consequences of them.

Table 2.1 *Power and principal theories*

Process	Power	Authors	Examples
Control through rewards and punishment	Higher teacher – lower pupil	Canter and Canter (2001) Dobson (2003)	Assertive Discipline Dare to Discipline
Negotiation and counselling	Power balanced	Dreikurs and colleagues (1990, 1998) Glasser (1969, 1992)	Discipline without Tears Schools without Failure
Therapeutic	Lower teacher – higher pupil	Gordon (1974) Harris (1969)	Teacher Effectiveness Training I'm OK – You're OK

Source: adapted from Wolfgang, 2005

In the middle of the continuum there is a balance with power shared and a democratic basis to the regime. No mention is made of teaching assistants and other support staff who, in the modern classroom, represent a growing source of power and influence. Their status, which is evolving, particularly through the development of the Higher Level Teaching Assistant, may well render such power continuums too simplistic.

When consigning the principal theories to a place on a continuum, key factors are considered such as who (pupil or staff) sets the limits, who dictates the agenda and what type of discipline exists or is imposed. At one end of the spectrum, the more authoritarian, is Dobson (2003) and at the other, Neill's (1968) *Summerhill* is often cited. Many contemporary theorists/educationalists in modern schools belong to a broad democratic centre ground, which has within it broad categories. Neither extreme represents a likely model for a school in the twenty-first century as an authoritarian approach is more likely to generate resistance than in a time when society was more hierarchical and teachers commanded respect by virtue of their status, irrespective of their skills. A casual and seemingly unstructured approach is not relevant in a society when qualifications, targets, inspections and accountability to public funding often drive agendas (Visser, 2000).

Working with many teachers undertaking a diagnostic questionnaire designed to illuminate which of the three groups they belong to revealed that very few belong entirely in one group. Some identify with all three groups, but usually tend to have a more dominant one, and a small number have a clearly dominant one. These members of staff are usually those who locate themselves in the 'Relationship/Listening' zone and they often work in more counselling or pastoral roles in their schools. However, the majority tend to associate themselves with 'Rules and Consequences' and 'Confronting and Contracting' seeing themselves as part of a broader system but also working with individual pupils. What the questionnaire reveals is that there is eclecticism in teachers' choice and also an expressed desire to probe theory more closely as part of professional discourse.

Systemic and solution focused approaches

Among the emergent themes of this book are the importance of policy and its link to practice as well as the recognition of the complexity of schools and the need for policy to have an impact on all aspects of the school system. The systemic approach acknowledges that complexity, context and the wider systems in which pupils exist (Ayers et al., 1995). Underpinning the idea of a systemic approach is the notion that when we reduce pupils' behaviour to its component parts we lose sight of the whole picture and the focus stays and is 'owned' by the pupil.

Human beings who share a common physical environment, such as a classroom, may not always interpret what an event means in the same way for reasons that are influenced by social factors (Molnar and Lindquist, 1990). The behaviour of all pupils and staff in a school or classroom in which problem behaviour occurs not only influences but is influenced by that problem behaviour. From this perspective a change in the perception of the behaviour of anyone associated with a problem potentially influences the problem behaviour. The following are broad implications arising from systemic approaches.

- It is important to understand the significance of context and pupil perceptions, and the views of others about that context.

- Behaviour originates from interaction between individuals, not from within individuals, and when pupils misbehave it is not in isolation.

27

■ Interactions can be conceptualised as 'simple', in other words determined by the immediate circumstances, such as the classrooms, corridors and playgrounds.

■ Interactions can be conceptualised as 'complex', in other words a specific incident or behaviour may be altered or modified by multiple factors, many of which have occurred outside the classroom or school, therefore in arenas over which staff have little or no control.

■ The cause of a specific incidence should be seen in terms of a 'cyclical chain of actions and reactions between participants' (Upton and Cooper, 1990) in which every factor can be interpreted as either a cause or an effect, depending on how we choose to 'punctuate the chain of events' (Cooper and Upton, 1990).

In applying this approach to classroom practice a series of questions present themselves.

■ What happens? Who is involved? When does it happen?

■ How do you respond and what is the usual outcome?

■ Why do you think they behave that way?

■ What positive alternative explanations are there for their behaviour? This is the crucial concept of 'reframing' that is a feature of this approach.

■ In the light of alternative explanations how could you respond differently?

■ What will you say?

■ What was the outcome of the reframing?

■ If successful, what changes took place?

■ If not successful, how will it inform your next reframing?

Source: adapted from Tyler and Jones, 2002

Systemic thinking recognises the intricate nature of the classroom and school behaviour and requires staff not to look for the simple cause and effect situation or to apportion blame – *'well what do you expect given his background?'* Instead there is a recognition that the classroom is a place where almost anything can happen and its unpredictability is all that is predictable. It is therefore not a place where staff can expect to have complete control and skills are developed to prepare for change, constant evolution and consider what worked last time but without the assumption that it will next time. The routines that are established help to secure the base shape of daily developments but the expectation of change is always there.

Solution focused approaches arise from consideration of a more systemic focus on behaviour problems and they are enjoying increasing success in schools in England and Wales. The following are the problems that help to lead to such approaches.

- Working with pupils can involve maintaining the *focus on the problem* behaviour that has taken place rather than looking to the future for solutions.

- Past *problems and failings are trawled over* and examined, problems are explained, and weaknesses and failings become the centre of discussion.

- There is an inevitable *urge to locate blame*.

- There appears to be *unwillingness in the pupil to want to change* and their self-identity seems to be centred on their negative role in the class fuelled by negative information from others, especially adults.

- The idea of *behaving well or appropriately seems remote*, unattainable and having little personal pay-off for the pupil.

Systemic theory illustrates the link between theory, thinking and practice and invites reflection of the assumptions of adults in dealing with behaviour problems as in SDE 2.1.

STAFF DEVELOPMENT EXERCISE
SDE 2.1 INDIVIDUAL OR SOLUTION FOCUSED THEORY

Consider whether, on balance, you agree with statement 1 or statement 2. The first statements indicate a belief in individual theories and the second that solution focused approaches might be more appropriate. Either way the statements usually lead to a wide ranging discussion and debate when ideas are shared in small groups and the links with practice and school policy are considered.

Statement	1 or 2
1 Problems in school are the fault of pupils, staff or parents. 2 Problems in school happen and are not caused by anyone's deficiencies.	
1 The problem is the behaviour of the pupil. 2 The problem is located between the pupil and the response of staff to their behaviour.	
1 The behaviour of the pupil will have to change. 2 The interaction, which is trying to resolve the problem, ends up maintaining it so it will need to change.	
1 Knowing the cause of the problem leads to the solution. 2 Knowing the cause does not necessarily lead to a solution and what sustains it could be the real problem.	
1 If the current solution does not work it needs to be repeated. 2 If the current solution does not work stop and try something else.	

Source: adapted from Porter, (2000)

Recent initiatives in England and Wales (Behaviour4Learning, 2005) have emphasised the potential for solution focused approaches for students in Initial Teacher Training. Based upon ideas developed by De Shazer and colleagues (De Shazer, 1985), they provide staff and pupils with an opportunity to orientate thinking and behaviour away from the problems of the past and 'reframe' them towards forward solutions, thereby moving beyond locating the problem and blame with an individual and seeing behaviour in the context of social interactions. They are based upon the idea that problems that pupils experience do not occur all the time – there are times, the exceptions, when all is well. The Behaviour4Learning (2005) guidelines suggest exception finding is 'an excellent foil' against negative labelling, such as 'naughty' or 'troublesome'.

A solution focused approach is about the identification of personal change that will offer a better life for the pupil, rather than change being imposed on the pupil because of the demands of others. In essence it moves the pupil's thinking from negative to positive and requires them to visualise what improvement looks like. Pupils are encouraged to see improvement in the long term but also to consider the best outcome in the short term and how this can be identified and achieved through their own coping strategies and strengths. The process of 'scaling' allows for the numerical notions to be developed in the pupil's thinking. Throughout the exercises in this book scaling is employed as it is useful in determining how bad or good a situation is but also nurtures thinking about progress, albeit incrementally. Many of the practices of solution focused thinking resemble those which apply to counselling such as the importance of empathy, openness and honesty, and emphasising that time given over for discussion is uninterrupted. The result is a sense of rapport and the pupil feels valued as a person rather than perceived as a problem.

Solution focused thinking can be applied to a variety of aspects of school life including curriculum matters such as reading (Rhodes and Ajmal, 1995), devising group based solutions as well as individual pupil solutions and, as discussed later, ways of improving classroom management for staff. It would be wrong to see a solution focused approach as a narrow, specialist time consuming therapeutic technique as it has much to offer the broader field of enhancing relationships in the classroom.

Table 2.2 *Stages of solution focused approaches*

Stage	Characteristic	Questions and comments
1: Other people's perspectives	Ask the pupil how others would recognise change.	'How will other teachers know how progress is being made?' 'What will other kids see you doing that is different?' 'What will your best friend notice?' 'What will your parents notice that is different?'
2: Exception finding	It helps to identify when the problem is not present or is not as evident and this can be an indicator of strengths.	'When was the last time it didn't happen at school?' 'When was the last time you did not react that way?'
3: Scaling	This can help break down the problem so it is not seen as so large that it cannot be resolved.	'On a scale of 1 to 10, with 1 being the worst things have been and 10 being how you want things to be, where are you now?' 'What tells you that you are on this point?' 'So what tells you that you have moved from 1 to _?' 'What would be a reasonable position to aim for next?'
4: Locating resources	This supports the pupil in the identification of personal resources that may work towards solutions.	'How have you dealt with the situation in the past?' 'What strengths have you shown before?' 'Who are the most important people that you draw upon for help and support?'
5: Coping	With children it is not always possible to locate times when problems have been overcome in the past. Identify how pupils are dealing with matters at present, which also indicates potential strengths.	'How are you dealing with things now?' 'What happens when the problem is not so bad?'
6: Stopping things getting worse	When the pupil cannot identify the exceptions (see Stage 2) it may be necessary to call in additional help/support or look to others to provide an initial coping device.	N/A
7: Providing constructive feedback	It is essential to keep pupils informed about what they are doing well, how their attitude is helping, and to provide evidence of their determination, imagination or creative thinking.	Provide feedback and ensure all sessions end with a constructive summary.
8: Ending	Make reference to the goals stated at the start and remind pupils of indicators of progress. Finish on time.	'Watch out for the miracle happening.'

Staff and solutions

The key principles which help create and sustain a solution focused approach might also strengthen professional practice for staff in school. The following outline reads like a positive guide for staff.

- Identify what practices work well and use these more often, providing of course that you have arenas within the school in which good practice is shared. By the same token, if it does not appear to be working then do not persist with the practice.

- By keeping focused on the future, change is more likely.

- Pupils and staff possess resources that can change classroom and school problems and their co-operation through a willingness to work together will enhance change.

- A big problem does not always require a big solution. Something small and incremental can stimulate considerable change, especially when once identified it generates hope and optimism.

- The behaviour is the problem not the pupils, who often see themselves as living, breathing problems in their own right.

It may even be useful for staff to draw upon the formal stages (Table 2.2) and to formulate similar questions for their own practice. For example, in seeking other people's perspectives: 'How will my colleagues know when things are going well?' In the case of exception finding: 'When was the last time I did not react that way?' or 'How have you dealt with the situation in the past?' For scaling: 'On a scale of 1 to 10, where are you now with that group?' and 'What would be a reasonable target to aim for?' and so on with other issues. The structuring, identification of success and utilising professional support can all provide an evaluative framework that can be adopted and used in teams.

Solution focused approaches have a value for staff experiencing difficulties in terms of behaviour with some individuals, groups or classes. In applying the approaches a member of staff might use the stages, or an adaptation of them, to examine their own behaviour in a reflective manner. However, it may be that a close colleague or mentor could be involved and both might utilise the framework to:

- reflect on what is happening and isolate areas of success

- make decisions about class management that scales current concerns and identifies solutions

- identify resources or personnel required to help meet targets

- set priorities that consider the long term, but also agree short-term success criteria that will be good enough.

Behaviour problems are rarely as simple as being totally pupil located. There are more benefits to be gained by addressing them using a multifaceted approach including how to reflect upon and enhance practice. However, introducing such an approach would be problematic in a school culture that operates in a more sanctions/punitive way. If not understood school-wide, it would be in danger of clashing with other approaches leaving pupils not knowing what is expected of them and staff committed to a solution focused approach feeling undermined.

At the end of this chapter you will have decided:

■ the degree to which theory will explicitly inform policy and practice

■ key theories or groups of theories that are linked to practice in the school

■ whether individual or solution focused approaches are compatible with the thinking of staff.

The positive framework of the school and classroom

In this chapter the positive elements that support effective behaviour management policy and practice are considered through the three 'R's: rights, rules and rewards. The accepted practices of praising pupils and reward systems are subject to close scrutiny and exercises provide opportunities to clarify thinking and practice on these crucial positive areas of behaviour management in schools.

The buttresses of school behaviour policies are the positive aspirations that are encapsulated in statements about rights, rules and rewards that the school see as essential to their success. These statements and the discussion that leads to them are as significant, indeed more significant, than decisions about sanctions that are so dominant in behaviour management and its expression in school policies. Kinder and Wilkin (1996) found that schools were good at stating their approaches to whole school sanctions but rewards systems in policies were less evident yet it is hard to see how the two elements can be disconnected.

Rights

Initial statements in policies often rightly cover the values, principles and mission of the school and these ideas will inform any articulation of the rights that students and staff possess. Chapter 4 includes a more extensive discussion of who possesses power in school. Here it is important to highlight that pupils today are more aware of their rights than their predecessors and often invoke them, not always appropriately, during heated moments. They may not always be expressed clearly but they exist and present challenges to teachers and teaching assistants who insist upon respect by virtue of their role, experience of life or status. Three key teaching principles on rights are worth considering.

■ Pupils need to be taught about rights and their link to responsibilities and how taking responsibility for their own behaviour is part of preserving the rights for all and, similarly, 'your right … is my responsibility' (Rogers, 1990).

■ Examination of rights can often lead to the realisation that they are common to both staff and students, particularly in the case of older pupils who are very aware of, and invoke, what they believe are their rights. The merits of this are that pupils are helped to realise that staff have their rights at heart and that they are shared.

■ Rights do not exist in isolation and as remote bland statements. They are linked to value statements made in policies and inform the rules that are devised or negotiated with pupils.

Rules

Schools create rules as an integral part of the behaviour policy and the means by which pupils understand school-wide boundaries and issues. They also provide a structure within which relationships can develop positively and reflect the ethos of the school. In order to be comprehensible and facilitate consistent application, rules need to be linked directly to rights, rewards and sanctions. Classroom rules developed by individual teachers, teaching teams or groups of pupils build upon the tone and content of the school rules yet add a flavour that may be unique to that classroom or subject.

It is helpful to distinguish between rules, which are consistently applied to all, and 'directions' (Wright, 2005), which are variable and apply to a given subject or context such as the distinctive directions that might apply in physical education or working in science laboratories.

There are many merits in having rules beyond that of providing boundaries.

■ They define what a particular school wishes to see as an expression of itself, what rights it embraces, what it deems to be good and what is desirable or undesirable. These are stated long before the rules that embrace them are constructed.

■ They are an articulation of the unity of the school and a manifestation of teamwork.

■ They create an opportunity for pupils to become involved in determining what is and what is not acceptable.

■ They meet the expectations of parents that there is an expression of order and the ethos of the school.

■ They help children, especially in early years settings, who have had differing upbringings and notions of authority to experience a single set of rules and a school climate and organisation which supports and enforces them.

■ They reflect the importance of ordering a society in such a way that individual rights are identified and preserved as are the rights of the society, and demonstrate that without rules it is hard for society to function.

Rules are a key part of any discipline plan but their purpose is often misconstrued. They help to ensure that punishment or sanctions are not arbitrary but linked to an agreed framework that all know. However, it is *not the breaking of the rule* that merits punitive action, whatever shape and form it takes, but the fact that something has taken place that is a human violation and an intrusion on basic social norms, values and rights. This is what should be linked to the sanction or consequence and the rule needs only to be used as reminder of the desirable behaviour. Being asked to pick up the litter in class as a sanction means little if the reason for it is seen as no more than breaking the 'litter rule'. However, it has significance if it is understood why the classroom needs to be litter free and how depositing litter in the wrong places causes environmental damage and is socially unacceptable. An examination of why anyone, adult or child, follows a rule usually arrives at one of three answers. We follow the rule because we have been persuaded that *there is no alternative* to the rule and have been manipulated by others into compliance, because we have been threatened by being punished therefore compliance is based on the *threat of the consequences* or because we *see the value of the rule* and that it is right, appropriate and needed for our sake and for our sake of others. If the latter is a valid aspiration then rules and the reasoning behind them need to be taught.

The development of rules

The process of creating rules will be linked with the other elements of behaviour policy and will mirror the commitment of staff to creating practices which complement the behaviour policy and reflect a desire for coherence and consistency. The Key Stage 3 Strategy (DfES, 2004) suggests that rules should be:

- developed with pupils
- clear, positive and enforceable
- expressed in inclusive language
- few in number, clearly displayed
- evaluated, reviewed and changed as necessary.

Consistency in the application of rules will also mean that they need to be an expectation over time and seek to maintain standards for all students. Consequences of breaking the rules, whatever form they take, should be applied consistently.

Building on the above criteria SDE 3.1 explores the many facets of rule deployment and review and provides a guide for school based reflection as well as individual staff consideration.

STAFF DEVELOPMENT EXERCISE

SDE 3.1 GUIDELINES FOR REVIEWING RULES

a In pairs, review current practice at classroom level through scaling to determine to what extent rules and explanations are valid and apply to your practice (10 means they apply all the time; 1 means they never apply).

b In a larger group or a whole staff group, discuss findings and consider what needs to be added or changed in the behaviour policy.

Rules need to be:	Explanation	Scale 1–10
Permanent	They should not be subject to variations throughout the day or lesson. 'Stay in your seats in lessons' may not be desirable for specific lessons and is therefore more a 'direction' than a rule.	
Positive	They should state what is required in a positive way as it is more effective to teach a desirable outcome than to eradicate an undesirable one. Avoid 'don'ts' as they do not indicate desired outcomes and it is hard to express negatively stated rules without portraying an authoritarian air.	
Explained and understood	They should be expressed in language that can be understood or explained. In the case of young children and at transition they need to be taught. A key term is 'respect' – it is important not to take for granted that all pupils understand what 'to respect' means (see page 40).	
Few in number	Keep the number of rules down to between four and eight. Long ponderous lists that few remember invite increasing opportunities for rules to contradict each other.	
Brief	Keep them as brief as possible. With young children give the rule a name, for example the 'walking rule' or 'helping rule'.	
Utilised and referenced	Make reference back to rules as they are not ornaments but live expressions of values and principles. Often devising rules is seen as an end in itself and laminated outcomes gather dust on the wall.	
Fair	While not always being able to practise it, pupils are attuned to the notion of fairness.	
Consistent	They need to be consistent with the values and aspirations of the school and with each other.	
Advertised and enforceable	The process by which *all* parties find out about them needs to be considered. They should be clearly displayed, which permits easy enforcement through reference to the rule.	
Written as observable behaviours	Rules should relate to observable behaviours so they are able to be reinforced. In the case of classroom rules, pupils need to become involved in a consideration of the detail and implications of the rules.	
Reviewed	They must be reviewed and, if necessary, modified or changed.	
Owned	Pupils need to realise that rules apply to the whole school and pupil involvement in development leads to increased understanding and sense of ownership. In addition, they are more likely to be seen as fair and worth abiding by.	

Schools have implicit rules (Allen et al., 1994) that seem just part of the natural working day and are taken for granted. Often they are habits that have arisen from practice and no one has ever seen the need to question them or had the temerity to raise the reasoning behind them. Any review of rules should look at whether there is a need to render them explicit and also whether agreed rules only apply to pupils. Rules gain in strength and credibility when they help to preserve the rights of more than the pupils and are seen as desirable as part of a genuine *whole* school approach and applicable to all. The alternative would be:

- Swearing is not permitted in the school except by Mr Cranky, the Caretaker, who does not know better.

- Pupils are given deadlines for handing in work but do not receive deadlines by which it will be marked.

- Everyone must walk on the left side of the corridor except the Deputy Headteacher.

'Respect our classroom' is a positively framed, if somewhat general, rule which demands extrapolation to avoid confusion, especially for younger pupils, and to incorporate behaviours which can be seen. The key word and the complex word is 'respect' and it is essential to discuss with pupils exactly what this means. For example, it might be interpreted as follows:

1 Hang up your coat.

2 Ensure that your shoes are not dirty before entering the classroom.

3 Enter quietly and go straight to where you will start your work.

4 Move around the class without disturbing others.

5 Ask before you borrow school or other pupils' personal equipment.

6 Seek permission before you go into anyone else's tray.

7 Keep the classroom tidy by putting things like books and equipment away and not leaving any litter.

Thank you.

Whatever the explicit rules, the requirements on pupils about how they function in a class can lead to many expectations that are expressed in regulatory form and are therefore rules in all but name. Wragg (1993) noted from interviews with teachers that rules could be classified under certain headings and these have been adapted for SDE 3.2.

STAFF DEVELOPMENT EXERCISE

SDE 3.2 AUDIT OF CLASSROOM RULES

Although not every issue is relevant, with other staff who work in the same classroom, consider questions a–c.

a Which areas from the list of issues below are covered in the classroom?

b Which are not appropriate?

c What areas that are not included in the table?

Issue	Notes
Talking: when it is permitted and when it is not	
Movement around the classroom	
Work-related: organising work and materials	
Safety matters	
Equipment/materials and how they must be used	
Social behaviour	
Clothing: both uniform and for specialist tasks	
Presentation of work	
Space: when the classroom is available and when not	

In the context of the advice given above about limiting the number of rules, the art of rule setting would seem to be getting the most messages across through the fewest statements with the highest level of understanding and pupil involvement in the process.

Whatever the rule, its success or otherwise is likely to be determined by enforcement factors rather than the rule itself, such as the tone adopted at the rule creation stage, probably at the beginning of the school year, which Rogers (1995) defines as the 'establishment phase'. Here the significance and purpose of rules become apparent. In practice compliance is more likely if staff adopt both tone and body language that expects it rather than demands it and remain calm throughout, repeating the rule if necessary. Another helpful practice is making reference explicitly to the rule and expecting compliance, for example: 'Jenny, you know the agreed rule for calling out in class – keep to it, thanks'. Wheeler (1996) demonstrated that pupils between 4 and 7 years of age could produce lists of what she preferred to label 'acceptable behaviours' rather than rules. In her research the pupils produced what amounted to a code of conduct in which each statement had an opening verb and then an explanation of the verb (the hyphens are added here). Therefore:

Walking in class – is safer for everyone.

Using a quiet voice – helps us to concentrate.

Talking nicely to each other – helps us make friends.

The verb + reason approach has much to commend in that it provides the easy memorised and referenced hook word – the verb – and the supportive purpose behind the rule. Wheeler also mentions how pupils, including some who attended the unit for emotionally and behaviourally disturbed children in the school, were encouraged to identify and celebrate positive behaviour in others. Her research into her own context confirms that pupil participation and ownership are crucial to any whole school approach and the language, as well as the rule, belongs to the student. What 'ownership' means is being part of the creation, accepting the rule, identifying with it and seeing the reasons behind it. The alternative of not involving pupils can make the rules appear imposed and reflect an authoritarian model, although acquiring or inheriting a difficult class may mean initial rules have to be set by staff. Even here, however, the promise of review and discussion can create involvement, albeit later. Ultimately rules are determinants of and reflectors of the climate in which relationships develop and are just part of the positive system which depends so much on individual pupil–staff interaction.

Praise

Celebrating success and achievement in class or school forms a natural part of the way adults interact with young people and with most of them it works well. Praising pupils seems to be an agreed feature of effective teaching (Behaviour4learning, 2006) and there is no doubt that many pupils react positively to good news about their progress.

However, deployment of positive labels on pupils who rarely hear such good news or, more significantly, do not possess a positive self-image can have the opposite of the intended effect. Telling a pupil that they are 'clever' or 'good' when their own experience tells them otherwise is likely to be a negative event. If it does not resonate with their experiences in life and their self-esteem, such praise can generate conflict which may be expressed in negative behaviour. The following suggestions licence celebration and contribute to the long journey of building a more positive notion of self.

- Give positive feedback privately and sometimes in written form, which suggests that it is not reactive but thought through and genuine.

- Give your verbal praise and speedily move away before the negative or self-deprecating retort can be given.

- Announce your intention in advance, for example stating, 'I would like to say something good about you (your work or your attitude)' and then add, 'would you like to hear it?' which, even if it generates a negative response, leaves the pupil to think about what it was that you might have said.

- Avoid the self-image issue by offering evidence that the work or behaviour has been positive for others. 'Helping Sara out has meant she will be able to finish on time. Thanks.'

- Positively question and then offer endorsement such as 'how did you work that out? You solved that problem pretty quickly'.

The importance of praising every pupil every day was stressed in earlier versions of Canter and Canter's (1992) Assertive Discipline approach. Apart from the logistics, the potential to devalue praise to the point that it may not even be noticed renders this idea problematic. It also raises a more fundamental matter – that of the value of praise in raising pupil self-esteem and helping to create a school climate that nurtures appropriate behaviour. *This is not an advocacy that praise has no value* but a recommendation that staff in schools should research and reflect on their use of praise and assess whether it is the best practice or whether encouragement may be more useful. Dreikurs et al. (1998) suggest that encouragement is the most important aspect of child-raising: 'it is so important that the lack of it can be considered the basic cause for misbehaviour'. A misbehaving child is one that is discouraged. Like punishment and sanctions, which are discussed later, the difference between encouragement and praise is not simple and that lack of clarity becomes exaggerated in the classroom setting. However, exploring and understanding the distinctions helps to illuminate the practical potential that encouragement may have. What follows is an opportunity aimed at beginning to separate the two notions and reviewing how such ideas would inform classroom practice.

STAFF DEVELOPMENT EXERCISE
SDE 3.3 PRAISE VERSUS ENCOURAGEMENT

Individually or in small groups, read and reflect upon the information below which distinguishes between 'praise' and 'encouragement' before discussing questions a–e. In larger groups or a whole staff group, revisit question e and agree any changes to policy and practice.

a How clear is the distinction between praise and encouragement?

b What are your views on praise or encouragement being used extensively?

c Describe cases of effective use of praise or encouragement that you have noticed?

d What are the implications of the difference between praise and encouragement for classroom practice?

e What are the implications for school policy?

Praise …	Encouragement …
Indicates to pupils that they have satisfied the requirements of others: 'You are worthwhile when you do as I wish and meet my standards'.	Indicates to pupils that they are able to evaluate their own performance: 'You are trusted to be independent and responsible. You do not have to be perfect – that you have improved and made an effort is the important thing.'
Can sometimes appear patronising in that it comes from someone in a superior position..	Can be seen as a facilitating message from equals.
Encourages an external locus of control in which pupil behaviour is determined by others and they are only valued when they meet the demands of others.	Encourages an internal locus of control in which pupils feel empowered from within to keep trying resulting in the development of self-confidence.
Focuses on outcomes and achievements only.	Focuses on the strength of their work, their effort and engagement.

The literature on the balance between positive and negative comment has resulted in a consistency of view that there should be more of the former than the latter and there is no disagreement with that view here.

> Policy should make explicit reference to how the school will establish a climate where praise and encouragement far outweigh the frequency of punishment and admonition.
>
> (DfES, 2004. 9:20)

What needs to be emphasised is that comments which are neither praising nor punitive, perhaps defined as *neutral*, tend to be about uninterrupted learning and more of these than any other should be an aspiration.

Corrie (2002) explores the difference between using praise extensively and using it selectively. When using praise *extensively* the teacher sees it as a valuable reinforcement of correct behaviour and makes no distinction between praise and encouragement. When using praise much more *selectively* there is a deliberate decision not to reward or offer positive comment in a way that can be seen to be false so it should only be given as recognition of genuine effort and achievement that pupils themselves would recognise. Here, the fundamental belief is that pupils behave well because they want to do so and not in compliance with what adults want to impose upon them.

The extensive or selective use of praise may well be polarised positions and, in practice, staff will operate somewhere between the two positions. Nonetheless, it provides another analysis that invites fundamental questions about the value of praising as a means of nurturing correct behaviour or enhancing self-esteem. Ultimately, if whatever is said to a pupil is to make any difference at all, it needs to register with their feelings and be recognised by them. 'I like the way that you worked so quietly this lesson, Joe' means little unless Joe realises it, agrees with it and recognises the difference his silence has made to his work – if he does not, the word 'I' is probably the only significant one in the statement.

Rewards

> Those schools with a strong emphasis on rewards also tended to have a system of sanctions that was perceived by the pupils as reasonable and just. When schools did not have a high level of consistency of practice, teachers' application of disciplinary processes was erratic and, at worst, quirky.
>
> (Ofsted, 2001, item 78)

This section asks key questions about the purpose of rewards in schools and then looks at reasons why they exist in *your* own school before making suggestions about the practical applications – given that use *is* made of rewards in your school. Although 'rewards' and 'sanctions' have been separated in this book their interrelationship cannot be overstated. One barometer is the formal written policy, although some schools have rigorous and altruistic documents that are not mirrored on the ground. Any review of current policies might begin by analysing the number of statements made in the average lesson that are positive and even celebratory, the number which are negative and focus on the critical and punitive based components, and the number which are neutral. Sometimes the driving force that leads to negative statements are expectations of parents and the demonstration of how tough the school is on misbehaviour for audiences outside. If the connection between policy and climate is to make any sense the positive–neutral elements need to dominate. However, several policies reviewed in preparation for this book offered little more than 'do that naughty thing and this is what will happen'. In most schools and in most professional development courses for teachers and support staff it is taken for granted that there should be a system of rewards, but even here there is an argument to be engaged in before consideration passes over to a discussion of reward systems.

The construction of the reward system will need to be as open and democratic as possible. It could be that those who believe in the value of rewards need to accept that there will be those who will remain outside the system while not undermining it or subverting it. Any system is more likely to work if there is commitment to it and if limitations and reservations have been shared. The question of staff who do not endorse the system will need to be addressed, especially the issue of whether the pupils who they come into contact with are going to be omitted from the scheme.

STAFF DEVELOPMENT EXERCISE

SDE 3.4 REWARDS ARE BRIBES OR ARE NATURAL

Opposing views on rewards invite a chance to reflect on what we see as their purpose. Are they bribes or a natural part of acknowledging effort and progress? In small groups, read the opposing views on rewards below and consider their positions before arriving at a justification statement, for example, 'we come down on this side because …'. Share the statements and consider the impact of these statements on current policy and procedures.

Kohn (2001)	Gordon (1996)
We (have) come to be seen as … goody dispensers on legs … rewards try to make bad behaviours disappear through manipulation. They are ways of doing things *to* students instead of working *with* them … . Schools will not become inviting, productive places for learning until we have dispensed with bribes and threats altogether.	There are a number of teachers who feel that 'bribery' will be the ruin of many a poor child. Coincidently though … many of these same teachers spend a good deal of time applying for promotions and pay rises or looking for opportunities to increase their status or kudos. The message seems to be … it is alright for me to seek a pay-off for what I do, but you're supposed to have an intrinsic love for the lessons I present to you.

One way in which staff can confront the reward issue is through examining the merits and problems of rewarding pupils, some of which will have emerged through undertaking SDE 3.4. On the merit side it can be argued that rewards:

- mirror the society in which we live which rewards the industrious and the talented, and pupils learn that being good, helpful, creative and working hard brings tangible results

- form a part of a culture that determines its own rules and accentuates positive responses to that culture, and help staff define the culture for the pupils

- provide pupils with choices – rewards help to break down aspects of behaviour into clearly understood segments within which pupils can make decisions

- have the capacity to create a climate of celebration – pupils enjoy rewards and they help to provide a motivator, especially for those in school who struggle with both work and behaviour

- are not bribery because bribery is a reward for dishonest or corrupt actions and not a privilege for achievement or effort (Riddall-Leech, 2003)

- are an expectation of society in general and governors and parents in particular – they help to provide a means of positive communication with parents.

On the debit side rewards:

- do little to reward the average and compliant pupil for they all too often go to badly behaved pupils who have been caught being good or have demonstrated improvement

- create an extrinsic motivation for pupils – they should work hard and behave well because they acknowledge the intrinsic value of doing so

- convey a model of staff interaction with pupils that is based upon a token system, not a strong supportive relationship – they devalue staff–pupil relationships

- are little more than bribes to pupils to conform. Pupils become dependent on the reward and do not see the value in making wise choices

- possess a built-in 'inflation' – the year starts with limited reward for the very best work and behaviour and finishes with extensive rewards for an increasing range of both work and behaviour

- foster a competitive ethos as pupils become rivals and occasionally become aggressive towards each other – in school or class based systems rewards mean winners and therefore losers, which is demotivating or nurtures competition.

STAFF DEVELOPMENT EXERCISE

SDE: 3.5 REWARDS IN MY SCHOOL

Complete the scaling component and then discuss conclusions in small groups before bringing them to the whole staff. Consider the following statements and scale their truth (a score of 1 means this is not true in your school; 10 means it is true) before reflecting on the potential impact on the behaviour management policy.

We have a reward system because it …	Scale 1–10
is expected by parents	
is considered important by the governors	
works for all pupils	
encourages independent learning	
provides a counterbalance to the sanctions we also have	
changes behaviour	
improves pupils' self-esteem	
provides staff with tangible evidence of improvement in behaviour	

Setting up a reward system

> Pupils confirmed that … they did not feel that rewards were used systematically or fairly.
>
> (extract from school policy cited in DfES, 2004)

SDE 3.4 illustrates just one of the arguments to be found in ideas and practices on behaviour management. Undertaking the exercise leads to discussion and debate that usually make explicit the strong feelings that people hold. It may be that this and other exercises lead to a major review of practice, if only to affirm current practices are working well. Of course it is natural to say that we want pupils to learn for learning's sake, to develop a passion for engaging in problem solving and seeking knowledge, and that rewards are not the sole motivation behind school, even though they have a key function in a competitive modern society. Similarly, from working in a variety of schools, it is apparent that staff express to pupils that their achievements and their efforts are valued and that they will be rewarded, and most teachers have a form of reward, either informal or formal, from the warm smile to the highly sophisticated star chart. The key question may not be whether there should be a reward system but how it will be deployed and how it complements the fundamental theoretical approaches adopted by the school. If it is a school or class in which behaviour systems are part of a controlling approach, the rewards will be perceived by the pupils (and others) as controlling (McLean, 2003). If they are about endorsing pupil autonomy, they are more likely to ensure that the behaviour rewarded will happen repeatedly.

The form of the rewards needs discussion between staff and with pupils, as does how they may be linked to specific achievements and their age appropriateness. In the main rewards fall into four categories:

- natural rewards, sometimes non-verbal, that occur as part of classroom interaction, for example praise, acknowledgement or smiles, and not always from the adults

- social rewards such as celebration in the class or school through assemblies, letters to parents, work displayed, a visit to the headteacher or a senior member of staff, or earning a whole class/tutor group reward

- object rewards such as small gifts, useful items for school use, badges or tokens

- privilege rewards such a playing a game, computer time or increased activity choice.

Although designed to motivate, rewards have the potential to have the opposite effect. For example, a token based system such as stars, stickers or even more tangible goods can lead to certain pupils being rewarded more than others. It presents the professional with another dilemma – do I ensure that all pupils receive a reward and make it available to all, thereby devaluing it since it is meant to be earned and linked to merit? Not all pupils appear to possess the capacity to respond to working and behaving for its intrinsic value and some may never develop it so need to be motivated by an external reward. Indeed it might be argued that the public examination system rewards only certain types of thinkers and learners and leaves the rest disenfranchised, given that they have failed to achieve the necessary passes that mean they are rated a success by school and national audits.

In schools two kinds of achievement are usually rewarded: good work and good behaviour, especially from those not often associated with good behaviour. Unless there is an insurance that most or all pupils gain something from the reward system, it can be demotivating for those who cannot access the system. For the pupil who finds it hard to gain rewards there needs to be a clear indication as to why they are given and how they can be gained, otherwise they fail to serve a purpose. This begs the question: 'what purpose do they serve and whose needs are met by them?' This is especially true of systems which reward effort as it is extremely complex to measure effort and yet many schools say they value and reward effort as much as achievement. I know of one school that used to celebrate both achievement and effort in a major annual event and pupils received tokens for both in all areas of the curriculum. However, the effect is somewhat tarnished when the value of the effort tokens was half that of the achievement tokens. Such events serve more as a public expression of the school and the majority of pupils have little connection with the event apart from an increasing cynicism about it.

It is the human element that often transcends any material reward. The immediate positive impact results from noticing and acknowledging the pupil and their positive behaviour or sustained improvement before anything more tangible is added. As one special school states in its policy … *the most effective and enduring rewards that we are able to provide are our attention, affirmation and approval. This is achieved by individuals in the classroom and through whole school assemblies*. However, when it comes to more concrete rewards it is essential that they are linked to behaviours that are made explicit so pupils know exactly why they have been given and what form they take. Once given, they *should not be taken away* no matter what happens thereafter. Through negotiation it is possible to ensure that a particular reward is something the pupils want, not what staff think they want, although all adults in the classroom must feel comfortable using it and that it can be earned speedily. As with most effective methods of motivating children either in work or behaviour, giving pupils a say in the system is likely to be more effective than imposing one on them. Giving pupils a choice of activity as a reward nurtures independence, although too much choice is not helpful where children are not used to it and find it hard to make good use of choice (MacGrath, 2000).

Evaluating the reward system

If a reward system is developed to help pupils improve their behaviour and motivate pupils, the following guidelines will help. Table 3.1 offers extended criteria for self-evaluation. Each of the criteria/arguments might be scaled 1–10 as undertaken in SDEs elsewhere in the book.

Table 3.1 *Evaluating the reward system*

Theme	Criteria/Argument
Internalising good behaviour	Regard rewards as part of a policy of internalising good behaviour and not a means of controlling pupils unless, of course, control is the purpose of rewards, which links to the overarching theories that help to guide the policy.
Does not disrupt learning	Ensure that the giving of rewards does not disrupt learning and that on-task behaviour remains unaffected. If they are given at the start of the lesson they will be in danger of being perceived as controlling and will detract from the main purpose of the lesson.
Getting the timing right	Link the reward with desired behaviour by rewarding as soon as possible after the event, especially with younger pupils for whom waiting a day means that the moment has gone.
Equality of experience	Ensure they are experienced by all, not just the able, the compliant and those who know how the system works! If only used by a few, the system demoralises the many. One way this can be overcome is by making rewards co-operative so pupils earn rewards for other pupils and for the whole class or school as well as for themselves. In that sense they may be linked to the mission statement of the school and to its core values.
Age appropriate	Consider age appropriateness both in terms of the reward and how it is given. For example, public pronouncements are not likely to be welcome by secondary school pupils or even older primary phase children.
Integrated and natural	The reward system should form part of an integrated approach and not be separate from other ways in which behaviour is managed. To that end, they need to be understood as a positive relationship approach and a natural component of a staff–student relationship.
Incremental	Value an incremental approach by making initial small rewards that are relatively easy to attain and gradually build upon these. The danger of large or frequent rewards is that by the end of the first term they have lost their potency and effectiveness.
Consistency	Ensure that there is consistency of application, especially if used by more than one class or member of staff within a class. Hill and Parsons (2000) noted that teachers who stated that their rules were applied inconsistently were not rated highly by the pupils.
Specify reasons	Specify the reasons so that it is clear why the reward is given and how others might gain such privileges, for example 'effort in …', 'mastery of …', 'improvement in …', 'supporting of …'.
Never taken back	Once given, no matter what behaviour ensues, never take a reward back as it devalues that reward. It *may* suggest that the reward has not served its purpose.
Link to effort and improvement	The temptation is to offer rewards for achievement only, often the most obvious achievement – a form of 'best in show'! Effort matters as much, if not more, and maybe other criteria for rewards could be mastery or improvement.
Nature of reward	Material rewards are not always the best ones, especially with older pupils. Sometimes, maybe often, a celebration delivered verbally can have more impact than a token, sticker or other item.
Explanation	Pupils need to know why a reward is given and what they did to earn it for two reasons. First, they will know that similar behaviour *may* have similar outcomes and it may need to be clarified if this is the case. Secondly, it sends a message to the class that this behaviour is valued by staff.
Variety of givers	All too often it is the teacher who decides who will and will not receive rewards. If they are an expression of clear and identified behaviours, other staff and pupils need to be drawn into the process.
Diminish learning	Any reward that takes pupils away from the focus on learning, the classroom environment or the school is in danger of cheapening and devaluing that learning.

STAFF DEVELOPMENT EXERCISE

SDE 3.6 RANK ORDERING EFFECTIVE REWARDS

a Rank the following in terms of their effectiveness – most effective first (copies of Table 3.1 may help deliberations). Any additional forms of reward may be noted.

b In groups, share the results, evaluate practices and consider the implications for practice and policy. In the discussion it would be an advantage if certain members of staff had already gleaned the views of pupils on these ideas.

Reward	Rank
Being given a token such as a star for the star chart	
Being invited to help another pupil	
Being openly praised for their good or improved behaviour	
Being praised by peers	
Being sent to the headteacher or other senior manager for praise	
Receiving a 'smiley face'	
Being asked to support or help another pupil	
Being given extra responsibilities	
Receiving a certificate of achievement	
Being singled out after the classroom activity has been stopped	
Receiving private acknowledgment of effort or improvement in behaviour	
Parents being informed by a letter	
Being allowed an increase in choice of activity	
Agreeing a formal contract with the teacher	
Receiving non-verbal messages of approval	
Being given less onerous tasks	
Parents being informed by a telephone call	
Being given material rewards such as prizes or tokens	

It is a natural corollary of any reward system that there should be an arena for celebration that is a coming together of the school or group of classes to highlight the achievement in behaviour and learning. These events usually have the additional function of providing an opportunity to deliver messages that apply to the audience. Assemblies are, in one respect, the outward manifestation of the success of the system and therefore given the advocacy of such an approach in this book, such celebrations are not to be decried. However, there are certain cautions that should be mentioned. First, they need to be a celebration of the different and exceptional. Of course, for some pupils with extreme behavioural problems normal behaviour might be both different and exceptional and therefore it merits consideration for reward. For the majority of pupils, however, there is a danger in being given a message that compliance, keeping to the rules and the normal expectation of behaviour merit celebration. Secondly, if it is to be a celebration, or even just an information session, beware of the impact of delivering negative information. I remember being invited to talk to a year group in a secondary school and, having spent considerable time preparing a session that was balancing the serious with the humorous and the entertaining with the informative, I found myself following a tirade from the Head of the Year on the defiance of certain, clearly guilty, pupils who had been flaunting regulations on smoking. The tone that I had wanted to generate would now be impossible and the messages that were to be conveyed unlikely to be heard as we all recovered from her address.

At the end of this chapter you will have decided:

- the degree to which the positive elements of interaction with pupils will be enshrined in the behaviour management policy

- the ways that pupil and staff rights will inform the policy

- the number, nature and good practice in the application of rules at classroom and school level

- the value of praise and how it is best handled in the classroom

- the structure and nature of the reward system and the way in which pupils will be rewarded.

The negative side: punishment to restoration

This chapter considers a range of approaches to dealing with problem behaviour in ways that inform policy and practice. Power, defiance and authority are considered as a background to an examination of whether staff administering punishment, sanctions or consequences offer distinctive and effective solutions or whether restorative justice, with its emphasis on pupils assuming responsibility for action and change, may offer alternative ways forward.

Who has power?

Before any examination of the negative aspects of behaviour policy a broader and deeper question about who really does possess power in classrooms needs to be considered. There has been an almost imperceptible shift in recent years in the powers that schools and staff within them possess in their attempts to create appropriate environments in which learning can take place. Power regimes within schools are constantly in a state of flux with increased devolution of choice to schools and a seeming decline in the powers and influence of local authorities. However, schools are subject to escalating bureaucracy and initiatives emanating from external agencies which, at times, give the impression of giving power to schools to directly carry out the wishes of an all-powerful centralised bureaucracy, rather than creating truly autonomous schools. Fundamental shifts in education policy, thinking and practice have taken place compelling the question: 'who really does possess the power in education?' In terms of the structure and management of schools, 'collaborative cultures', 'leading from the middle', 'flat hierarchies' and other similar concepts all question the traditional structure of schools and suggest shifts in power together with changes in teachers' and other staff's roles and identities.

With regards to pupil behaviour in classrooms and schools, staff sometimes relate that there have also been developments and questions about possession of power might also apply here. This can be reflected in ways in which misbehaviour is handled by staff.

There seems to be a continuum of approaches to dealing with the negative side of pupils' behaviour which extends from the deployment of punishment to inviting pupils to make amends for their actions and seeking their own solutions to the problems they cause for others and themselves.

Recent years have seen the development of classrooms in which pupils are being invited to have an increasing say. Once the arena in which teachers determined all the planned and guided activities and the discipline environment, there is a gradual shift to pupil participation beyond learning. All-powerful teachers now invite, nurture and encourage pupils to make decisions and to assume responsibilities. There is a growing recognition that staff have *influence on* the classroom through acknowledging that they are exciting, sometimes turbulent, places where there is a need to be adaptable and responsive to random events, but they do not have *control over* the classroom in the sense of ensuring that everything functions in a predictable, regulated and, it could be argued, sterile way. External forces, such as imposed curricula and centralised, perhaps, politicised, determination of what is deemed to be good practice, have had an impact on the power of teachers, as has the influence of parents and the growing number, significance and status of teaching assistants. If these views are an accurate reflection of reality, how schools manage such shifts and how consistent they are in their application of changes of practice would seem highly significant. There is no doubt that, for better or worse, since the mid 1980s there has been a major shift in teachers' and teaching assistants' power and status, but how embedded in practice this has become needs consideration.

STAFF DEVELOPMENT EXERCISE

SDE: 4.1 POWER IN SCHOOLS

a Undertake the scaling operation by reflecting on your school or classroom and determine whether you concur that 'old style' is still in operation – score 1 – or the 'new style' is firmly in place – score 10. If this style, in your school or classroom, is somewhere in between, suggest an appropriate score.

b Compare the results with your colleagues. It may be helpful if one person analyses groups by ages of pupils worked with or compares results between teachers and teaching assistants.

c Consider the implications of the findings for behaviour management.

d To what extent do teachers operate in the new style but resort to the old style when threatened or when it is easy?

e What are the implications for pupils, if any, of a member of staff who operates inconsistently across the spectrum?

Issue	Old style	1–10	New style
Learning and teaching	Teachers determine the planning and organisation of the lessons.		Pupils influence, even determine, how learning and teaching will be conducted.
Discipline	Sanctions and discipline are solely determined by teachers.		Pupils are invited and encouraged to exert self-discipline and make decisions on behavioural issues.
Power	Teachers have total power and manage by dominance.		Pupils' autonomy is encouraged and management is through support and guidance.
Rule generating	Teachers create the rules and tell pupils about them.		Rules are developed by the pupils who are invited to own them.
Rule breaking	Consequences of breaking rules are set by teachers, are inflexible and apply equally to all pupils.		Consequences of breaking rules reflect the influence of all pupils, the difficulties faced by the rule breaker and contextual information.
Rewards	Teachers determine the nature, frequency and allocation of rewards.		Reward systems are negotiated with and agreed by pupils.
Support	Teachers are supported by a select group of pupils – the 'monitors'.		All pupils play a role in supporting the teacher and each other in the classroom.
Teaching assistants	In carrying out their role teachers are aided by teaching assistants who carry out their wishes.		Pupils' learning is supported by teaching assistants who participate in planning lessons.
The door	Once the door is closed teachers dominate the classroom. Few outsiders are admitted.		Outsiders are invited into the classroom and they participate in the learning process. The door is open to those who enrich learning.

Defiance and authority

Pupils sometimes carry with them the baggage of their history of oppositional behaviour and some even carry the baggage of the cause of their behaviour problem, for example lack of appropriate parenting. Attached to these pupils are labels of being 'anti-school', 'anti-authority' or simply 'naughty'. Teachers and teaching assistants belong to an authority group who possess the power to label negatively but instead may choose to offer praise, care and warmth. Exposure to adults who value their ideas and seek to positively enhance their notions of self is not easy for pupils who exist in a negative twilight. They sometimes reject the positive because they are not used to it or secure with it and being anti-authority is easy for them as they aim to manipulate friendly adults into the enemy camp. In doing so, they maintain their own image of the world. After all, they believe that the current understanding and kind disposition of staff is temporary – and they may be right – and, sooner or later, it will be replaced by attempts at strong discipline, so why not speed up the process? It is so easy to resort to traditional binaries of rebel versus authority figure, rewards versus blame and praise versus punishment. When faced with misbehaviour acted out publicly it is extremely difficult for adults not to take the challenge personally. Indeed sometimes it sounds as if it is personal and, occasionally, it is! In the end professionals are faced with a decision either to resort to conflict-based approaches based upon power that resides in their role or to maintain, sometimes frustratingly, a caring stance which seeks to bring about change in pupil behaviour, albeit often incrementally. Asserting the power that resides in the traditional roles of adults in schools may create compliance but usually does little to help pupils and their learning environment.

Defiance is then a response that affirms the image that is given to pupils by significant others. In heated moments labels are ascribed to a pupil and they respond with behaviours that ensure the accuracy of the label. Calling a child 'naughty' or 'rude' may well lead to behaviours that live up to the label, hence the oft heard advice that encourages *pupils' behaviour to be labelled but not pupils themselves*. It is natural that authority figures, such as teachers, react to defiance and feel threatened by it, but it is easy to forget that it is often a natural response especially during certain phases of life. For example, the 2-year-old child, having learned to walk, talk and engage in all forms of communication, learns the word 'no' from adults, particularly in dangerous situations, so perhaps little wonder that it becomes a natural retort when their own status is threatened. Similarly, in adolescence new found physical and mental abilities and increasing potential capacity to make a difference to their world leads many to be defiant as they attempt to extend boundaries that teachers, parents and society impose. Defiance is also a natural response for those older people or those struck with debilitating illness as there grows a reliance on others to fulfil tasks that were once simple and straightforward and with dependence come frustration, anger and low self-worth. Defiance is not the property of a few but something we all engage in at times.

For many staff in school nurturing, empowering, encouraging and caring are more comfortable aspirations than conveying the negative authority that is often associated with the role. However, there is no choice when the carefully selected rules are broken, as schools, like any other social unit, are governed by rules that help in the fulfilment of its aspirations. Nonetheless terminology deployed in schools often reflects the continued use of 'punishment' and little use of 'consequences', although it is important to emphasise that the language that schools adopt will be significant in portraying how they deal with troublesome behaviour and rule breaking. To help to distinguish between the key terms which occupy the rest of this chapter, what follows is an attempt to define 'punishment', 'sanctions' and 'consequences'. It is highly likely that in schools they are terms that are interchangeable but it is important to explore their differences as they provide staff with different opportunities and lead to different outcomes.

Punishment requires the pupil to be treated in such a way that it is *deliberately unpleasant* to have broken a rule or misbehaved in some way. Power and authority come from the member of staff and the chosen task:

■   is not predictable

■   may not be consistently applied to all similar 'offences'

■   is not directly linked to the behaviour

■   is the personal choice of the member of staff.

Sanctions imply a link with *specific misbehaviours* and the outcomes of non-observance of a rule. They are related to the implementation of rules and are not personal but form part of a more formal management policy which means they are predictable and consistent. Power and authority come from the policy and system it supports.

Consequences are linked directly to the misbehaviour and demand that the pupil recognises that link. They follow *naturally or logically from the behaviour* and, like sanctions, form part of a more formal management policy which means they are predictable and consistent. They offer the opportunity for power and authority to come from the pupil's engagement with their own behaviour and the formal system.

Punishment

One of the crazy things about human nature is that if we are doing something, and it doesn't work, we do it more, we do it harder and we do it more intensely.

(Brandes and Ginnis, 1990)

'Punishment' is a term still commonly used in schools but becoming less so in the education literature. Arguments for its continued use are often based upon familiarity and tradition – we all know what we are talking about and we are all used to using it. It has a long association with the world of law and order and is a manifestation of the power of those who administer the law – authority – over those who break it – criminals. However, as a term, and in its application, it may not be the most appropriate approach for a school in the twenty-first century. Nevertheless, there is a case that might be made for its continued use.

- It is a term known by all and an approach expected by many, including parents, some outside agencies and the media.

- It offers clear messages that certain behaviours are not acceptable.

- It meets the needs of some adults, usually for revenge and a feeling of reassertion of control.

- It offers a balance for the emotions aroused by the negative behaviour of the pupils.

Before any dismissal of punishment, it is worth considering the emotions that are aroused when someone close to a member of staff, for example their own child, is bullied. Occasions and events can arouse such passions that the rational side declines and outrage and the need to deal with the culprit take control. Some offences committed in schools, for example drug related or violent in nature, demand quick, decisive action to protect the school and its pupils. When considering terminology in relation to these kinds of problems, 'sanctions' and 'consequences' could also apply but they lack the connotations carried by 'punishment'.

Wilson (2002) argues that there should be emphasis on the *form* of punishment. He adds criteria for determining what form might be chosen which can be summarised as acknowledgement, shame and deterrent.

- Acknowledgement: the wrongdoer needs to be alerted to what they have done wrong, why what they did was wrong and the impact that they have had on others.

- Shame: the wrongdoer should recognise that what they did was wrong and feel shame or guilt.

- Deterrent: the punishment has sufficient impact; in other words it is unpleasant enough to outweigh the temptation to repeat wrongdoing.

Wilson (2002) also argues that to have a negative attitude to punishment may have 'disastrous consequences' and uses bullying as an illustration of why punishment is necessary. Included in his arguments are that punishment functions as a deterrent, encourages compensation for victims and makes the bully fully conscious of their actions. In choosing bullying he is dealing with an issue that staff in school find themselves dealing with as a third party. They are not usually directly involved until they notice the bullying or it has been drawn to their attention and they are required to be both judge and jury for an act which is complex and difficult to resolve. Blame is such an emotive issue in the case of bullying and the passions aroused can impose themselves negatively on attempts to bring about changed behaviour and develop 'support groups' rather than apply blame (Robinson and Maines, 1997; see also www.luckyduck.co.uk). Wilson calls for a consensual approach and 'not something arbitrary and tyrannical' but his single deployment of the term 'punishment' (and not 'sanctions' or 'consequences') to incorporate all responses to misbehaviour may inadvertently create a negative feel to the argument.

In the day-to-day behaviour management in school staff engage not only in relationship issues such as bullying but also in less aggressive threats such as those to the good order of the school, disruption which runs counter to their intentions for the lesson.

59

These usually less emotive incidents need consistent handling and positive action but whether 'punishment' best describes that action is debatable. Given that the most common negative behaviours reported by staff do not fall into the major event bracket but more into the downright irritating category, punishment would appear to have limited value as the chosen term and approach. Among its negative attributes it:

■ demands payment for mistakes but does not require change in behaviour

■ can resemble bullying: 'if you do not change, this aversive behaviour will be carried out against you'

■ can involve anger and generates a desire for revenge thus providing a poor model for the resolution of conflict

■ generates emotional distance from those who, despite outward appearances, often need emotional closeness most

■ focuses on actions of the past that cannot be changed or undone

■ makes no requirements of pupils to do something about their behaviour, except be passive recipients of the punishment

■ tells pupils what they should not do, but not always what they should do

■ emphasises that they have no control and that power and control, and perhaps abuse of them, rests with staff

■ fosters resentment

■ can waste a lot of time – other methods are also demanding of time but may bring about change.

Whatever the chosen route for dealing with difficult behaviour the inclination to punish can be strong and, as with any area of the policy, the methods and the language need to be set in the context of the aspirations of the policy. Research evidence is helpful in informing the discussion. It is not surprising that Harrop and Williams (1992) discovered pupils in primary schools did not agree with their teachers about the effectiveness of specific punishments but both groups agreed about the effectiveness of parents being informed. It is important to reflect on whether just because one group, staff or pupils, see a certain punishment as ineffective that it will always be so. For example, Harrop and Williams (1992) also found that 'being told off in private' was considered much more effective by staff than by pupils. Teachers' sensitivity to not wishing to openly chastise a pupil or damage fragile self-esteem would mean that this is the preferred choice over more public and severe techniques and it is difficult not to agree.

Whatever the arguments displayed in SDE 4.2 it is helpful to reflect upon actions that are seen as effective and to share views. What follows in SDE 4.3 provides that opportunity and the experience would be enhanced if the views of pupils on these ideas had already been gleaned through classroom research.

STAFF DEVELOPMENT EXERCISE

SDE 4.2 CLARIFYING THOUGHTS AND BELIEFS ON PUNISHMENT

Having read the above arguments, in small groups discuss the arguments for and against punishment. In the light of the discussion select your favoured statement from arguments 1–3 and offer your reasons for the choice or, if none match your views, complete option 4.

Argument	Your reasons for selection
1 Punishment is the best way forward as it reflects our society and meets the demands and aspirations of the world outside.	
2 Punishment has strengths and weaknesses – at this stage in our development of the school I would like to look at alternatives and see if they have more to offer.	
3 Punishment is not relevant to the ambitions of this school and professional. I feel that there must be better ways of dealing with misbehaviour.	
4 Alternatively, I should like to suggest …	

STAFF DEVELOPMENT EXERCISE

SDE 4.3 EFFECTIVE PUNISHMENT

Scale each punishment in terms of its effectiveness: 1 for the *least* effective and 10 for the *most* effective. Compare your results in groups and also with the views of pupils. Add your own suggestions for 18–20.

Punishment	Scale 1–10
1 Being told off in front of class	
2 Being told off privately	
3 Being told off in front of the whole school	
4 Being sent to another classroom	
5 Being sent to the headteacher or other senior manager	
6 Being made to stand in the corridor	
7 Being sent to time out	
8 Being given extra work	
9 Being kept in at break	
10 Being kept in after school	
11 Being moved to another place in class	
12 Parents being informed	
13 Being made to finish work at home	
14 Being stopped from going on a school excursion	
15 Being denied a privilege, for example after school leisure activity	
16 Being given onerous tasks	
17 Agreeing a formal contract with the teacher	
18	
19	
20	

Sanctions

'Sanctions' seems to be the term increasingly used in schools although perhaps, as one member of staff suggested in a professional development session recently, it is simply the old term 'punishment' in a new guise. The term implies a link with troublesome behaviour and the outcomes of non-observance of a rule or expectation. A school which structures its behaviour policies around rules would naturally employ sanctions or, perhaps, the 'consequences' of breaking rules.

Sanctions, like punishment, help to set the tone of expectation of schools for the broader culture in which they exist and they represent a fallback position for those, both inside and outside education, who place responsibility on pupils for what goes wrong in the classroom and the school. There are three criteria that inform any assessment of the effectiveness of sanctions.

- Appropriateness: do they match the misdemeanour, and through them will the pupils link the adversity they face with the behaviour?

- Effectiveness: do they have the aversive effect that they are designed to have for the pupils concerned and, perhaps, on the other pupils and the classroom climate?

- Transformation: do they bring about the change in behaviour that is intended?

Sanctions can be a short-term effective way of dealing with personal anger, resentment and threats to power and can simply help adults feel good, provide an instant control 'fix' and reassert authority. However, they have many disadvantages, which could also apply to punishment, and it is important to consider whether these outweigh the merits. Sanctions draw attention to the surface behaviours but do not look to the cause and are short term once the immediate impact has died down. They emphasise the negative rather than promote positive behaviour. In doing so, they are unlikely to change pupil behaviour or attitude but may promote strategies that ensure they are not caught in future. They can also easily cultivate resentment, especially if unjustly targeted, and critical comments or reprimands can have the effect of reinforcing and supporting the inappropriate behaviour rather being a punishment (Algozzine and White, 2002). Sanctions, when applied harshly, have a contradictory nature to approaches to learning in that when pupils make errors in their work educators seek to show them where they might have gone wrong and may explain matters again using different methods or materials, in other words they seek to help pupils understand what was wrong and how to respond effectively. Behaviour correction based on sanctions lacks these positive elements. Finally, it is useful to have a rule reminder which helps to depersonalise the sanction. However, there is a danger in linking sanctions to rules as it gives a message that it is the breaking of rules which is the misbehaviour when, as stated previously, the focus should be *on the behaviour itself* and its impact on others.

Staff often agree with the above arguments and then convey that sanctions and punishment are an expectation of society, parents, senior managers and even pupils themselves. Apart from an awareness of their limitations, such as those mentioned above, if staff use sanctions they need to ensure maximum effect (see Table 4.1).

Table 4.1 *Criteria for the examination of sanctions*

Issue	Explanation
Linked to policy	Sanctions need to be consistent with wider school policy and this should be emphasised as they are being administered.
Connected to the level of the misdemeanour	It is important to be consistent with the misdemeanour in terms of the level and nature. A major infringement of behaviour policy which incurs a minor sanction demeans the entire policy.
Decrease disruption rather than increase it	Often the administration of a sanction can cause more disruption than the original offence and therefore correct timing matters a great deal.
Self punishment	Ensure that staff do not end up punishing themselves such as by losing precious break time. Sometimes sanctions involve staff getting involved in a spiral that generates further problems. They may assume a size and importance that far outweigh the original offence and leave staff chasing to ensure that the sanction has been undertaken.
Fair and just	Sanctions need to be seen as just by others *and* the involved pupil and they should not apply to those who were not involved. The problem here is often that pupils nearby may have taken no action but their inertia makes staff feel that they have been complicit and therefore merit the sanctions.
The final act	Sanctions need to be used carefully and without resentment, ensuring that once served the 'slate is wiped clean' and does not cause further problems. For example, punishing someone who has bullied another pupil should not put that victim at risk of further bullying.
Be negative	Although obvious, there are occasions when sanctions are applied but contain no negative element. They should not be something that resolves a short-term need of the member of staff or is pleasurable for the pupil, for example staying in a warm classroom on a cold, wet day.
Consistent	Sanctions should be applied consistently and to all pupils who commit the same misdemeanour.
Ensure closure	Once the emotional climate is right, closure through a debrief in which staff and pupils consider what happened and how it has been resolved is helpful. A reminder of the link between the offence and the rules that it infringed helps to depersonalise the event and the consequence of it.
Policy review	Sanctions should be reviewed in the light of the behaviour policy and how pupils feel about them. Continued monitoring of their efficacy ensures they serve their function as an expression of justice and fairness and as a part of a broader school policy.

One subject not raised in the above table is whether sanctions should be hierarchical, in other words whether there should be a 'scale' (DfES, 2004). The advantage of this approach is that pupils realise where they are in terms of numbers of misbehaviours and that repeated offending will lead to a higher level of sanction. The downside of linking sanctions to numbers of offences is that pupils' negative behaviour can be at the minor, irritating level and have little or no impact on others, but it can also be very serious and a major disruption. For this to receive a similar sanction because it may be a first offence undermines the idea of linking sanctions to the misdemeanour. Forms of sanction scale such as first offence 'yellow card' but second offence 'red' means that the 'yellow' one may function as little more than a warning and may not be taken too seriously and the whole notion of proportionality to the offence has no meaning.

Consequences

One of the principal writers and educationalists associated with logical or natural consequences has been Rudolf Dreikurs. Forty years ago he wrote that 'punishment today is still retaliatory rather than corrective in nature' (Dreikurs, 1968) and it is worth considering whether thinking in schools has moved on from this supposition. Clear delineation between terms is not always easy but is crucial. Although discussed earlier in this chapter, the fundamental criteria which distinguish consequences from punishment need to be pursued a little more. Consequences, be they 'logical' or 'natural', need to be:

- ■ employed in a reasonable manner that is also respectful

- ■ related to the behaviour, not the pupil

- ■ motivated by a desire to teach pupils about their behaviour as opposed to 'teaching them a lesson they will never forget'.

They are an example of where argument, in the form of a consideration of two ways of managing discipline, can inform practice. Exploration of the difference between consequences and punishment reveals five main areas.

1   **Social order: Consequences** are linked to the social order and the rules governing life that pupils need to learn in order to take their part in society. The pupil receives the message that they can be trusted to respect the rights of others in the school. As a result, pupils learn respect for their peers and staff, coupled with an understanding of their situation, even if they are not always in agreement with them. **Punishment** represents the power of authority and the arbitrary power of adults who are in authority which gives pupils the message that they must do as they are told by adults who know better. Resulting from this could be the adoption of an anti-authority stance, securing ways of avoiding being caught and general deviousness.

2   **Relationship to behaviour: Consequences** are logically related to the misbehaviour, which allows pupils to be helped to understand that the connection

between their action and the outcome is not connected to moral judgements and they are not being judged as good or bad. Misbehaviour is considered a mistake rather than a sin! The emphasis is upon the choice of the pupil and the member of staff's belief that they will make the right one next time. Distinguishing between deed and doer and never labelling a misbehaving pupil but staying focused on the behaviour conveys that they are worthwhile although some things they do give cause for concern or are unacceptable. The result, for the pupil, is that they feel valued, can make choices to improve their behaviour and come to realise that learning from experience is important. **Punishment** is more arbitrary and the pupil is labelled and thus receives the message that they are unacceptable and are bad, which in turn generates a need for revenge for the hurt caused. They also pick up that they are not liked and they will be shown who is in charge.

3   **Time difference: Consequences** are concerned with the present and what will happen now and not with atoning for past misdemeanours. They display a confidence in pupils being able to make decisions for themselves and understand the outcomes of what they have done or might do. **Punishment** concerns itself with the past and judgements about the pupil connect with the past so they feel that not only have they done wrong, but they have always been a wrongdoer. The result is that pupils believe that they are incapable of making decisions and of controlling their own behaviour.

4   **Emotional quota: Consequences** are delivered with a voice that conveys that there are clear reservations about what has been done but also genuine concern and even humour and affection. This results in the pupils hearing that what they have done is not liked but they are still okay, and that the world is not a negative place so they can feel secure within it. **Punishment** is characterised by a tone that is harsh and angry and displays a lack of respect for the pupil and a resultant feeling that they are not liked or respected, which may lead to a desire for retaliation, rebellion or feelings of guilt.

5   **Authority position: Consequences** provide options for pupils by giving them choice and convey the message that it is the pupil's decision and it is hoped that they make the wise one. The aims include giving responsibility and not engaging in conflict and authority is shared or can move from staff to pupil. **Punishment** demands compliance and conformity, and therefore conveys a lack of trust and faith in the capacity of the pupil to make choices. It does little to generate respect.

One of the main practical advantages of consequences is that they are linked to specific behaviours and possess a transparent logic for all to see if not agree with. They therefore take some of the stress out of behaviour management because they are not associated with the teacher's *personal* response to a specific pupil. As well as depersonalising the response, consequences apply to all, invite review should the consequence not lead to improved behaviour and, like rules, can be displayed for reference. They can be structured hierarchically, although cautions about this have already been mentioned.

In the development of consequences the logic becomes more transparent if pupils are involved in linking what will follow if a rule is broken, but it is crucial that staff also see that link and feel that the consequences are appropriate and fair for all. In most cases it is obvious what is needed but some serious behaviours, such as physical assault in anger, may be less logical. For these the immediate application of consequences may lead to increasing emotions and the pupil's anger could override any attempt to apply logic. It is essential that reference to consequences is made in a matter of fact manner that does not fan the flames that such situations almost inevitably produce.

Schools that adopt consequences need to be prepared for the potential impact that what can be seen as a radical approach will have, especially if the school has been used to a strong punitive regime. Parents and pupils may see it as a 'soft option' or think that negative responses to misbehaviour are being abandoned. As with all innovations, staff need to support the use of consequences by building a review into the process. Review is important and sharing practice is essential to ensuring consistency, and support for each other by sharing what works and does not work will help to create that consistency. At the formative stage it will prove helpful to involve the pupils in considering potential consequences so they can see why they are often described as 'logical'. Involving pupils does not detract from the ownership of the final decisions, which rests with the staff who have to deploy them. Not all misbehaviours have a natural or logical consequence and these behaviours require specific consequences, as will some of the more serious offences. Like other innovations these may not work well at first. If that is the case, consider revising the consequences. So much of effective behaviour management is about helping pupils to make wise choices and consequences help to nurture their own sense of responsibility.

STAFF DEVELOPMENT EXERCISE

SDE 4.4 CONSIDERING CONSEQUENCES

As individuals or in small groups, undertake a, b and c before returning for a debrief with the whole group. Look at the list of behaviours below.

a Consider whether you see them all as problems (they are all from various *genuine* behaviour policies).

b Although pupils need to be involved in the practice of consequences, it is useful to have your own perspective. Try to assign *appropriate consequences for each behaviour* by linking the behaviour and the consequence.

c Would pupils in your class or group find assuming more responsibility for their behaviour a problem? If so, how might you encourage it?

1	Constantly leaving seat when not required to do so
2	Leaving class without permission
3	Spitting
4	Talking out of turn
5	Possessing illegal substances (drugs/alcohol)
6	Tapping a ruler
7	Threatening other class members
8	Shouting out in class
9	Making put-down comments to other class members
10	Refusing to follow instructions
11	Being rude and disrespectful
12	Passing notes
13	Lying
14	Swinging on chairs
15	Play-fighting
16	Chewing gum or eating in class
17	Causing damage to school equipment
18	Constantly turning around
19	Throwing litter on recreational areas
20	Wearing outdoor coats in class

It is important to remember that the effective use of consequences when dealing with misbehaviour removes a major force for stress for staff, that is engagement at an over personal level, as it invites pupils and/or the system to take that burden. Potentially it decreases the number of occasions when teachers interrupt their own lessons with angry responses, get embroiled in heated or emotional exchanges, or exhibit negative energy that can distract non-involved pupils. Compare the language and the tone required for the following statements:

Example 1

'Karl, I see that by throwing the paper on the floor you have chosen to tidy the room later.'

or

'Karl, what are you doing throwing litter on the floor? You make sure you pick it up right now and see me at the end of the lesson.'

Example 2

'Your constant talking out of turn Jenny means you have chosen to leave the room for two minutes.'

or

'Jenny, I have warned you enough times about talking out of turn. Get out the room now and wait outside until I consider you can return.'

Like any form of response to misbehaviour, consequences are not without their critics (Kohn, 2001). Mention of them provides an opportunity to examine their validity, to adapt consequences to counter criticisms or simply to decide that consequences have no place in *your* school. There are three concerns. First, it is sometimes difficult to distinguish between traditional punishments and consequences because, ultimately, both involve a member of staff requiring a pupil to do something negative. It may well that the only difference will be the tone of voice adopted, which, in itself, may not be a bad thing! Secondly, consequences lack the harshness of punishment and should be administered respectfully, but the behaviour or task that follows may be logically suited to the offence which could still be harsh, thus the message received is a mixed one. Finally, over-application of the 'logic' element leads to pupils undertaking tasks linked to their offence that resemble punishment. Exercise 4.4 occasionally leads to strange, contrived, even draconian, responses, hence the criticism that consequences are punishments but dressed up in a gentler guise.

Whatever the criticisms, the calmness, the involvement of pupils in understanding their misdemeanour and the logic of it may offer a new direction in thinking that has potential benefits. The creation of a framework behind which staff can unite offers consistency, but being united within a singular framework should not mean that staff suppress individual teaching style and techniques. Rather it means that they function within a given, agreed and sophisticated framework that allows that which makes them an individual as an educator to emerge. Opportunities for long considerations of behaviour are not likely to be during a lesson but at times, made explicit, when only the involved students are present. Interrupting lessons is often necessary, but it is important to remember that adding the emotional heat of reprimand can mean that the staff intervention causes more disruption than the original pupil problem that it was meant to solve.

Restorative justice approaches in schools

One way of dealing with misbehaviour or with pupils exhibiting problems that is enjoying consideration in schools is restorative justice. Like the solution based approach mentioned in Chapter 2, it invites pupils to take increased responsibility for their actions and seek solutions. Restorative justice continues the aspiration of this chapter to seek the value in moving from staff administering punishment to pupils assuming more responsibility for their own behaviour.

Restorative justice approaches challenge many conventions and attitudes of western society that are based on punitive responses as the answer for misbehaving. They are based upon the idea that children face those who have been affected by their behaviour. These approaches are often associated with the criminal justice system, but in recent years they have become influential among those seeking to change ways in which problem behaviour impacts upon school communities. In terms of the criminal justice system Zehr (1990) talks about the shift from retributive justice to restorative justice as a 'paradigm shift'. Application to behaviour management would also require a major journey although restorative approaches already have an influence on support group techniques employed to deal with bullying (Pikas, 1989: Robinson and Maines, 1997) and comparable paradigm shifts are possible with this aspect of behaviour management (Lee, 2004).

The importance of restorative approaches for behaviour policy lies in the fact that the pupils and staff, not immediately involved in but affected by the behaviour, have a role to play in supporting those involved and helping to arrive at an appropriate outcome. The shift away from a conventional punitive regime to one based on restoration, in other words making good the damage done to personal feeling as well as property, recognises that the learning and school experiences of many pupils will be affected by the event. In these cases, in restorative justice terms they have the right to explain how they were affected by what happened and to influence resolution (Hopkins, 2002). The key person in this approach is often a 'mediator' and when their role is examined the connection with staff undertaking effective circle time or conferencing is apparent.

Mediators in restorative justice:

- respect the perspective of all involved

- are non-judgemental and impartial

- display empathetic listening skills

- display good questioning techniques

- invite and encourage solutions and do not impose their own

- aim to develop rapport among those involved

- are caring and patient.

Hopkins (2002) draws upon a case study of the application of restorative justice in a school context in which misbehaviour is perceived primarily as an offence against human relationships and the violation of the rules of the school is of secondary significance. Staff in schools demonstrate many of the skills cited above on a daily basis but not always all of them and they sometimes fall into the blame trap through their phrasing or body language. However, there is a growing use of conferencing in schools to resolve problems with pupils taking lead roles and more schools are engaging in peer mediation with pupils becoming mediators.

STAFF DEVELOPMENT EXERCISE

SDE 4.5 RESTORATIVE REFLECTIONS

In small groups, consider the qualities of restorative approaches in the left-hand column and note in the right-hand column whether they demonstrate comparative skills when dealing with misbehaviour in schools. Share findings and implications with the main group.

Restorative approaches	Notes
Respect the perspective of all involved	
Are non-judgemental and impartial	
Display empathetic listening skills	
Display good questioning techniques	
Invite and encourage solutions and do not impose their own	
Aim to develop rapport among those involved	
Are caring and patient	

There are certainly problems in the development of restorative approaches in a whole school community.

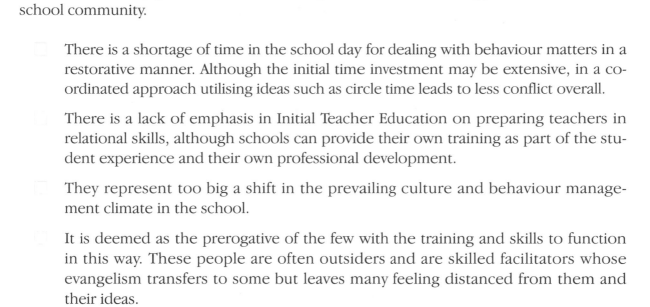

There is a shortage of time in the school day for dealing with behaviour matters in a restorative manner. Although the initial time investment may be extensive, in a co-ordinated approach utilising ideas such as circle time leads to less conflict overall.

There is a lack of emphasis in Initial Teacher Education on preparing teachers in relational skills, although schools can provide their own training as part of the student experience and their own professional development.

They represent too big a shift in the prevailing culture and behaviour management climate in the school.

It is deemed as the prerogative of the few with the training and skills to function in this way. These people are often outsiders and are skilled facilitators whose evangelism transfers to some but leaves many feeling distanced from them and their ideas.

Their potential is *probably* linked more to personal offences and serious misdemeanours than to the day-to-day management of groups and classes in school.

Whatever the choice of response to misbehaviour, professionals in schools will need to address whether they wish to improve behaviour or cope with it and what approaches are likely to achieve this. While Chapter 2 advocated that eclectic approaches to theory would have benefits for staff, some theories do not reside well with each other. Restorative approaches cannot form part of a regime in which punitive approaches are practised as the premises that underpin them cannot co-exist (Macleod, 2006).

The journey from punishment to restorative approaches sees movement from the more arbitrary, adult imposed to the more collaborative, socially determined. Whatever the chosen approach or approaches one fundamental question presents itself: 'which is most likely to bring genuine change in a pupil's behaviour?'

At the end of this chapter you will have decided:

the value of punitive approaches in serving the needs of the school

the overarching approach to dealing with negative behaviour

whether there is a link between the aspirations, values and mission statements of other policies and the chosen approach.

Influence in the classroom: the skilled adult

This chapter begins by reflecting on how to identify good practice that helps to prevent behaviour problems. The beginning of a career in the classroom, the importance of determining the climate at the beginning of the year and lesson beginnings are covered before finishing, naturally enough, with exits!

Earlier discussion focused upon issues related to the changing role of schools and the shifts in power that may be taking place in classrooms. It is in the classroom that the strength or otherwise of a behaviour policy becomes manifest through relationships with the pupils and the classroom management skills of the adults. If a behaviour policy is a document and no more then it is limited in scope, but if it is a live expression of the values, hopes, aspirations and practices of staff then one key area that needs to be shared is what practices and ideas are seen as helpful in preventing and dealing with disruption. These ideas may or may not find a form of written expression in the policy but they are an accumulation of the skills of all the staff and they certainly need to be stated and shared somewhere. They are divided into two. First, there are the daily actions of staff themselves in the turbulent world that schools can be. These are sometimes almost taken for granted as they may prevent disruption without the conscious awareness of staff that they are doing so. One classroom constant is the potential that adults possess to intercept misbehaviour. Like any preventative approach, this is hard to identify and impossible to measure; it simply happens through the everyday habits of good practice. These habits need to be identified, discussed and celebrated. They are the positive side to the classic 'I don't have any trouble with her' statement and the equally unhelpful 'he has dreadful problems with the Year 5 group'. Self aggrandisement or demonising colleagues is counterproductive and unprofessional; sharing good practice is the opposite. The second set of skills, considered in Chapter 6, are the methods employed to deal with disruptions and misbehaviour. These may vary between individual members of staff but again there needs to be agreement and sharing as part of the professional discourse.

Reflections on experience

One common feature of staff in schools is that all of them would have had experience of being a school pupil at some stage in their life and have memories of what, in their opinion, worked and did not work in their own school. It could also be useful to reflect on their current professional experience. These memories may well influence how they see others and how they would like to be in school. Working with teachers in professional development settings reveals a paucity of opportunities to consider 'what kind of teachers I have come across who were inspirational' (or the opposite), 'what kind of teacher I aspire to be' or 'whether I am the teacher that I want to be' and even fewer chances to express them. This is strange given that generating whole school policies would seem to require key members of the staff to consider how they stand in relation to important issues and in the teams in which they work. This is the opportunity to reflect on more than the competent and begin to look at the outstanding. Since it is only in recent years that there has been a rapid expansion in teaching assistants/support staff in schools, the focus is on teachers in SDE 5.1 which is a key part of a consideration of what it means to be a skilled adult in the classroom and it would only take minor modifications for a version for teaching assistants to be developed.

In the modern classroom it is rare not to find teams of adults working alongside each other and teaching assistants have become an integral part of the landscape of schools today. Their ideas and practices influence classroom management practices and they play a crucial part in preventing and dealing with classroom problems. As part of the preparation for this book, when forty teaching assistants from one secondary school were asked what three behaviours or approaches of teachers helped (a) to prevent disruption and (b) to deal with disruption, they were clear in their responses. Regarding preventing disruption the top five answers were:

1 consistency

2 well-planned, interesting lessons

3 respect for pupils

4 establishing clear boundaries

5 calmness.

On the subject of dealing with difficulties, which is the focus of Chapter 6, there were significant similarities:

1 consistency

2 calmness

3 being clear about and following sanctions

4 maintaining respect

5 being firm but fair.

STAFF DEVELOPMENT EXERCISE

SDE 5.1 PRECIOUS AND NOT SO PRECIOUS MEMORIES

Complete questions 1–9 and then share conclusions in a group. It is not intended that anyone should see answers to question 10 as this is a piece of self-reflection.

From your experience of teachers when you were at school and/or with whom you have worked professionally in the past ...

1 What kind of teacher really inspired learning?

2 What kind of teacher rarely inspired learning?

3 What kind of teacher created a warm, welcoming classroom?

4 What kind of teacher created a cold, unwelcoming classroom?

5 What kind of teacher rarely experienced disruption in lessons?

6 What kind of teacher usually experienced disruption in lessons?

7 What are the common characteristics of answers to 1, 3, and 5?

8 What are the common characteristics of answers to 2, 4, and 6?

9 Would you think it helpful to make a statement in a policy about the kinds of teachers you aspire to be in your school? If 'yes', what would you say?

Private self-evaluation

10 Reflecting on your answers, which characteristics do you possess and which do you wish you possessed?

Consistency, calmness, respect for pupils plus clarity of learning intention and response to difficulty all emerged as key attributes. However, consistency is yet another word that is often used with assumed meaning. It is used in this book to mean staff consistently challenging pupils' behaviour that runs counter to the values of the school which is likely to include racist comments, wearing inappropriate uniform, bullying and throwing litter. It could be said to mean consistent application of the will of the headteacher or consistency in the application of a certain sanction to a specific behaviour, which completely denies the need for flexibility and professional interpretation.

Positive adult role models

Any long-term consideration of resolving behaviour difficulties in schools needs to reflect upon how the adults in the school themselves behave and what expectations they transmit to their pupils. One of the main themes of this book is the importance of staff sharing and agreeing practices in a dynamic, collaborative culture. However, it is *not* suggested that everyone should behave in the same way but that there should be discussion focused on what adult behaviours and expectations are likely to achieve the best results.

SDE 5.2 provides an opportunity for reflection and self-evaluation for members of staff as a role model. Table 5.1 is a slightly adapted model of empowerment devised by Gordon (1996) who contrasts the two belief systems that teachers can set up and that could equally apply to support staff. They are cyclical in that the beliefs and actions 'feed' each other.

RESOLVING BEHAVIOUR PROBLEMS IN YOUR SCHOOL

Table 5.1 *Positive and negative models of staff attitudes*

Positive model (Empowerment)	Negative model (Disempowerment)
Staff possess a strong belief system including that difficult behaviour *does not mean* impossible behaviour.	Teachers possess a strong belief system including that difficult behaviour *means* impossible behaviour.
They take action.	They take action.
They expect success.	They do not expect success.
They draw upon personal resources, skills and potential.	They draw upon limited personal resources.
Their action is congruent with beliefs and this communicates an expectation of *success*.	Their action is congruent with beliefs and this communicates an expectation of *failure*.
They expect appropriate behaviour therefore they often see it.	They expect troublesome behaviour therefore they often see it.
Therefore positive results reinforce their belief system.	Therefore negative results reinforce their belief system.
Staff possess a strong belief system including that difficult behaviour *does not mean* impossible behaviour.	Staff possesses a strong belief system including that difficult behaviour *means* impossible behaviour.

STAFF DEVELOPMENT EXERCISE

SDE 5.2 SELF-EVALUATION: PRESENCE

Reflect upon the statements in the table and make a personal rating of between 1 and 10, 1 being the lowest. State your major celebration (and give a reason) and your principal concern (and give a reason). In larger groups or as a whole staff, significant discussion is likely to be about areas of agreement and ways that areas could be moved forward.

Statement	Scale 1–10
I convey optimism, confidence and have high expectations.	
I possess a coherent set of beliefs and values suitable for work with pupils.	
I link my actions to those beliefs and values.	
I have high expectations of success when taking action.	
I expect rather than demand appropriate behaviour from pupils.	
I believe that difficult behaviour is not impossible to manage.	
I believe that difficult behaviour is not impossible to change.	
I maximise the potential of pupils both as individuals and in groups	
I have something special about me, not included above, which is ...	10

P Resolving Behaviour Problems in Your School, Paul Chapman Publishing © Chris Lee 2007.

There can be no better way to influence behaviour in schools and classrooms than to be a positive role model: full of enthusiasm for learning, humorous and serious when appropriate and seemingly unflustered by the stresses of the classroom – and, at the end of the day, still a bundle of energy! But it is not always like that and, not being perfect, the next best approach is to be aware of preventative practices and good working habits.

Classroom procedures

No matter how well embedded the rules network in the classroom and throughout the school is, the rules need to be harmonised with effective classroom procedures and routines (Algozzine and White, 2002). The following model of the lesson and the school day suggests the four key elements of the lesson for which thoughts, practices and procedures are required:

1   starts: getting pupils in and starting work

2   learning: the core of the lesson

3   relationships: getting on with the pupils

4   endings: summary, goodbyes and exits

Stages 2 and 3, which are represented here as distinct and separate, highlight an interesting dilemma. It would appear from the list that learning comes before relationships, but others have urged the focus to be placed on relationships rather than results (Hook and Vaas, 2000). Such a divide, sometimes symbolised in schools with their academic and pastoral systems, understates the perpetual interchange between learning and the social, emotional and behavioural components of the classroom. The significance of the emotional aspects of learning to success in schools has recently been at the forefront of modern educational thinking. Successful pupils appear less inclined to misbehave and pupils who feel emotionally at home and possess high self-esteem are more likely to achieve. The complex interplay between results and relationships means that they are not separated here. Although the focus throughout is clearly on behaviour, learning is integral which means that no distinct discussion on learning and relationships follows but the entrance and exit stages still require consideration.

Starting the year

Whatever skills, attitudes and other attributes staff bring to the classroom there are routines that help to establish patterns of work and behaviour. These routines need to be instituted at the start of the year because, once in place, many of the behaviour management problems will be with pupils with whom a working relationship has been developed and therefore levels of intervention can be gauged and differentiated in accordance with that relationship. Rogers (2002) describes three basic phases:

1 the **establishment** phase in which staff determine the initial classroom tone through the development of routines, relaying or negotiating class rules and indicate how support is given

2 the **consolidation** phase when routines and climate may become modified in ways determined by staff

3 the **cohesive** phase when pupils take a more active role in routines and rules and correction takes place in the context of relationships between staff and pupils.

In many respects it represents moving from a model of staff power to shared power and from 'this is my classroom' to 'we all work here and have a job to do'. Speed of movement through the stages is linked to variables such as preconceptions about staff among pupils (their 'image'), staff personal circumstances, the chemistry of the class and many other factors. It is important that there is a desire to reach the 'cohesive' phase with the professional skills of all staff working in tandem towards that end.

On a tangential note on beginnings in classrooms, student teachers and newly qualified teachers are often given the advice 'don't smile until Christmas', which not only predetermines the timescale of the journey beyond the 'establishment' phase but offers a somewhat austere Dickensian model of the teacher as humourless and lacking in feeling – surely *not* key tenets of a good working relationship. If such advice is designed to suggest that no member of staff can assume that working relationships are immediately established, it has some limited validity. The skill that needs to be developed here is to know when to smile and how it helps to nurture positive responses. So many staff, teachers and teaching assistants enter the classroom with an unconscious competence – they are good at what they but do not necessarily know why or the theory behind it. For such individuals Christmas must come early!

Advice for the class for year/semester/term starts includes:

■ setting out expectations for the period

■ making clear your preferred teaching style or communication style

■ establishing routines, especially entry and exit

■ setting or negotiating class rules and publicising them alongside the consequences of broken rules

■ locating resources that pupils have access to and agreeing when and how they have that access.

The above are stages that are clear to identify and put into practice if deemed helpful. Less easy to deconstruct into its component parts is an attitude that sees behaviour management less in terms of control and more in terms of understanding, caring, supporting and facilitating. Being controlled is usually resented by adults so starting by feeling that the sole purpose of working with pupils is to establish control may be the foundation of establishing resentment as the initial reaction. Often it is advice from others that sets the climate and the individual member of staff may feel the need to adopt the norms of a controlling regime that dominates over their own more nurturing teaching and supporting style.

STAFF DEVELOPMENT EXERCISE

SDE 5.3 ADVICE FOR NEW STAFF AT THE BEGINNING OF THE JOB

In small groups, respond to questions 1–3. The session co-ordinator leads collation of all information and a member of staff will agree to use the information and advice from staff to write a 'good and bad advice guide' for staff. The following are initial questions for consideration.

1 What advice on behaviour management were you given about starting in your role in this school or any previous school that proved helpful?

2 What advice on behaviour management were you given about starting in your role in this school or any previous school that proved useless?

3 What advice would you give a new member of staff regarding behaviour management issues?

Leaman (2006) suggests, somewhat lightheartedly although there is a sense of underlying gravity, that there are five types of styles of teacher to avoid being. They are the:

1   dragon: ultra strict, creates cold atmosphere, is hated by able pupils and feared by the vulnerable

2   mouse: lacking in confidence and control, even experiences behaviour problems with motivated able pupils

3   pupil's friend: desperate to be liked and putting popularity before professional practice, ends up without respect from pupils and unable to make necessary learning demands

4   foe: a joyless individual who seems to hate children and young people and to perceive them as the enemy

5   uncommitted: likes the steady income, wishes they were somewhere else and has no interest in professional development.

While these appear extreme stereotypes, individual staff who exhibit some of the traits associated with them are unlikely to contribute positively to a coherent behaviour policy.

Lesson starts

The problem of lesson beginnings is usually more acute for secondary schools with their numerous lesson changeovers, but changeovers of subject matter can be just as challenging for early years and primary school settings.

Lessons start long before pupils arrive. First, the planning stage is crucial and thought can be given to any potential behaviour issues arising from specific individuals or tasks. The danger with pupils who are occasionally or often involved in behaviour that disrupts is that staff believe that they bring that 'baggage' with them to every lesson and a self-fulfilling prophecy comes to fruition (Wearmouth, 1997). Problems are expected and dutifully arrive on time from the predicted sources. Being aware of difficulties is helpful but singling out pupils for early intervention may not be the best plan. Secondly, the environment into which pupils enter needs thought to ensure sufficient lighting, ventilation, space and heat are provided as well as suitable well-labelled and accessible materials. Approaches to support, for example peer and adult assistance, also need to be part of the plan.

One of the dilemmas that schools, particularly secondary schools, face is whether the lesson begins in the corridor outside the classroom or on entry into the classroom. It is certainly the latter in terms of the learning process but the tone is often set earlier if communication and correction takes place in the corridor. In essence it is about whether pupils line up outside the classroom or whether they walk straight into the lesson, but it also makes broader statements about who is in charge of the classroom and illustrates that arguments in education are often as much about day-to-day procedure as they are about theories. In terms of consistency it is helpful if staff have an agreed position on this as establishing the habit of lining up can mean it becomes a short process.

STAFF DEVELOPMENT EXERCISE

SDE 5.4 TO LINE UP OR NOT TO LINE UP

Read through the opposing arguments below and discuss them with a colleague before answering questions a–d.

a What additional arguments to either case do you think apply?

b Regardless of current practice in your school or classroom, consider which set of arguments best suits your own professional views?

c What broader statements does it make, if any, about approaches to pupils?

d Do you agree that there should be consistency in the application of this process? Give reasons for your views.

Arguments for lining up outside the classroom

1 It allows teachers or other staff to set the tone and make a statement about the lesson.

2 It indicates that the lesson begins with the permission of the adult.

3 It makes statements about whose classroom it is.

4 It allows for any potential problems to be dealt with and means that minor matters of order and discipline stay outside the classroom.

5 ....

Arguments for going straight into the classroom

1 It permits arrival at a more leisurely pace and avoids the rush to desks.

2 It avoids the potential for conflict developing outside which then enters the classroom.

3 It makes statements about whose classroom it is.

4 It is more adult and mirrors the real world – where else do you queue outside except for a sale?!

5 ....

It seems obvious that being in the classroom at the outset helps start the lesson (Rutter et al. 1979) and, although seemingly a simple, if not trivial issue, it is part of the professional relationship with pupils and colleagues (McManus, 1995). Nevertheless, discussion with teachers and teaching assistants reveals that they are often distracted, not by highly significant issues that require immediate attention but by more trivial matters that could have waited, which presents challenges when reprimanding pupils for their lateness! Agreed, consistent and shared procedures mean that, if there is more than one adult attached to the classroom, one can be 'distracted' and the other is able to carry on.

Establishing the learning environment

Just as such a seemingly innocuous everyday act as lining up outside classrooms has arguments for and against and can reflect more than a simple act, so too lesson starts represent a time when all can go wrong and discipline can be lost. Advice on lesson starts includes:

- avoid registering the pupils – it can be long and ponderous and can be done later

- determine where you will stand – near the door to control entry is one popular option

- say that special hello to pupils who you have been worried about

- have an activity already prepared that everyone engages in at the start

- have the lesson or day plan set out for all to see

- ensure that all members of the staff team know their role.

Wragg (1984) observed how experienced teachers greet pupils, keep them central to their vision and start when there is silence. Eye contact matters as much as voice. Staff develop what Rogers calls 'preferred practices' from which core classroom management routines emerge and these are divided into two key areas. First, there are the ways of responding that match the tone, values and practices suggested in the whole school approach to managing the classroom. Secondly, there are the personal values that each member of staff holds and hopefully has made explicit and which blend with the agreed practices. Stress for teachers can result where one or two staff deploy practices that contradict those of the agreed policy – assuming it was agreed – or worse, where two colleagues such as teachers or teaching assistants work in the same classroom but employ incompatible techniques underpinned by values that are not complementary.

Endings and exits

Like starts, endings represent a crucial phase of the lesson, especially if pupils are moving to another lesson and therefore may take their disruption with them. The significance of recapitulation of main themes needs stating, but if pupils need time or are totally engrossed in their activities it may be no more than cursory. A more significant problem is the early finish but this can be planned for through well-established routines such as:

- all pupils having on-going tasks or projects to which they return as a matter of routine

- quizzes that recap key information

- questions about the next lesson which establish the knowledge base of the class.

Exits demand similar practices to entrances such as voice, body language, securing a clear order of departure and the power of a smile as well as a chance to celebrate the lesson and pupils' involvement in it and short reference to the next lesson.

At the end of this chapter you will have decided:

- best practices of classroom practitioners that you have known

- key features of good starts to a career, a year and a lesson

- key features of the conclusion phase of the lesson.

Interventions: principles and practices

In this chapter the emphasis is upon intervening when disruption is occurring in the classroom, although many of the ideas are also relevant to problems that occur in other areas of the school. The initial focus is on broad ideas such as assertiveness, a different view on conflict and systemic approaches before moving on to the 'micro' skills, the responses to disruption as they occur. Here the attention is on staff behaviour and reaction and this is divided into initial, further and final interventions which ultimately lead to exclusion from the classroom.

The significance of action in schools having a theoretical connection, especially if that theory is founded on research into classroom practices, has been underlined in Chapter 2. Before detailing ideas on everyday practices and skills that help determine the outcome of behaviour problems there is a consideration of some broad ideas and theories. Discussion with staff in a variety of roles in schools has revealed that, through engagement with the literature on behaviour management, they see purpose in the theory/practice link, they understand the bigger ideas behind them and they will apply some of them in their schools in ways that complement other practices in the school. However, what is sometimes the case is that the responses of staff can be reactive and inconsistent, and this approach is not the result of a thoughtful understanding. Their reaction to disruption is not part of the discipline plan, is often disconnected from the systems so painstakingly constructed in the policies and is symptomatic of the view of the classroom as a place of stress and turbulence.

Whole school rewards, rules, sanctions, encouragement and praise are all designed to take the stress from adults and avoid over-emotional engagement when difficult situations arise. An expectation for pupils to behave and staff and pupils to support each other is a natural corollary of agreements, expectations and systems that have been agreed and are consistently applied. However, even within the context of well-established and rigorously applied policy, behaviour management techniques are still crucial, not only in dealing with difficulties but also in preventing escalation of minor problems. Whatever approach is adopted by school or adult in the classroom, the need to enhance personal skills and expertise is central because when pupils are being defiant or confrontational the capacity of staff to draw upon responses that deal with the situation is essential. Before considering these responses it is important to restate that they need to synchronise with or form part of the school policy, the approaches adopted by your colleagues and your own personal values. They are not solutions but ingredients that help to formulate your repertoire of classroom approaches. They are the 'micro' skills that relate to the 'macro' picture but they are not answers in themselves. If genuinely part of your professional style and a reflection on the culture in which you work, they are likely to work for most people most of the time but, if they are just one individual's approach, they may work for some people some of the time.

The clash of personal values with the culture and prevailing climate of the school can be a source of stress for staff. Corrie (2002: 114) observed that student teachers reported that, during their school practice periods, they adapted speedily to the values and attitudes of staff in school, even if they fundamentally clashed with their own values and they ended up sounding like the teachers with whom they were working. It is essential that staff approaches blend in with the school's and that they feel comfortable with the prevailing practice and culture, especially in terms of transmitting a coherent approach to behaviour to pupils. When they do not, the danger is either psychological withdrawal and subsequent stress or they simply feel a compulsion to leave. Transparency and a capacity to embrace diverse views in a *coherent* policy that everybody, pupils included, understands helps to secure compatibility of individual approaches and whole school policies.

Assertiveness and conflict

One thing that will not work, apart from giving a certain amount of short-term relief for the adult, is the behaviour battle as school staff end up paying the 'toxic penalty'. Staff engagement in behaviour battles with pupils runs the risk of their being viewed as an enemy, the logical consequence of which is to decide to 'get tough with them to teach them a lesson'. Applying such logic to adult behaviour is a good way of learning lessons – would adults refuse to do what others want them to do? The outcome at best would be resentment so getting *tough* is not a good option but getting *smart* is and assertiveness is one way of doing this.

Assertiveness offers the language of confidence and respect in exercising control. As Rogers (2004) points out, it includes body language and, in acquiring assertiveness skills, staff need to consciously control the messages that they want to convey in their body language. 'Presence' is a hard to define attribute of effective classroom practitioners but those who possess it often exhibit the attributes of the assertive. Examination of Roger's (2004) list of 'key principles' of the language in relation to classroom management reveals the influence of both the language and skills of assertiveness and conflict resolution.

Discussion with teachers and teaching assistants reveals how important it is to be assertive. This is neither a recommendation nor a rebuttal of ideas of the specific technique of Assertive Discipline (Canter and Canter, 2001) but rather an endorsement of assertiveness as a way of being and a response to disruption in the class. Assertiveness is often a misunderstood term and there are misconceptions that it is self-orientated and preserves the individual's rights no matter what (Hall and Hornby, 2003). Assertiveness is about confidence, clarity of approach, engaging in and asserting basic rights and assuming responsibility for those of others. It produces no winners or losers but affirms rights, and the rules that embrace them, including the right to learn and to teach.

The alternatives to an assertive response to troublesome behaviour are as follows.

- **Direct aggression** gets rid of a lot of frustration in the short term but is stressful in the long term and damaging to relationships. It fuels negative conflict, disrupts those nearby (and maybe further away) and is not a good role model.

- **Indirect aggression** is characterised by sarcasm and 'put-downs' and has the potential to deflate pupils and damage self-esteem. It emphasises superiority and ensures insecure relationships.

- **Passive aggression** is exemplified by being manipulative and it encourages self-pity. It aims to control people by making them feel they have to acquiesce to needs in order to maintain a stable emotional climate.

Assertiveness can be seen as an attitude that informs behaviour; perceiving conflict differently can also have a positive effect. Conflict is an inevitable part of life and has the potential to be highly negative and destructive, but it also can be positive, leading to enhanced understanding and a feeling that views have been aired and solutions arrived at.

Positive conflict has problem solving at its core, allowing various different perspectives to be explored in the search for an outcome that meets group and individual needs. Through a willingness to listen, understand and be flexible the focus remains on issues not people, the behaviour and not the person. The outcomes are improved communication, innovative thinking, affirmation of relationships and a sense of shared responsibility. There are no losers but there is moving forward, problem solving and change. Such a description could well apply to a perfect lesson!

Negative conflict is emotionally charged in an atmosphere where individuals may feel threatened and blame is attached. Negativity is expected and often achieved through aggression, personal attack, rigidity of stance and ill-informed opinion. The outcomes are resentment, hostility, deterioration of relationships, loss of self-esteem and further problems generated rather than resolved. All of these are not dissimilar to how many adults react when under pressure. Imagine that you join a group of your peers on a training course. You are presented with a challenge that you know you are not able to do well or that you feel embarrassed about. You are afraid that you will be publicly exposed as not being able to achieve what others can do and some seem to do with ease. You are then faced with a choice of adopting 'bad' behaviour or being seen as stupid. Which do you choose? Certainly, the 'bad' image has greater prestige attached to it than the stupid one and it is not surprising that pupils will choose the former when faced with failure.

Staff can adopt behaviours that fan the flames of conflict, indeed light the initial match, and what determines whether the conflict will be positive or negative is rarely the conflict itself but likely to be how people respond to it. Table 6.1 demonstrates how behaviours and attitudes that are potential sources of negative conflict can have positive outcomes if interpreted and handled differently.

Table 6.1 *Negative conflict or positive outcome*

Subject	Negative	Positive
Contest	Argue and generate a contest.	Look for solutions that are win–win.
Audience	The pupil has an audience of peers or adults who provide active or passive support or are perceived as part of the accusatory gang.	The audience are part of the solution and an arena of help. The pupil is removed from their audience or the situation is dealt with later.
Lying	Accuse of or infer lying.	Value the truth even though it may have negative consequences.
Volume	Shout at the pupil and get the last word.	Remain reasonable and communicate at conversational level with no anger and little emotion.
Insults/ grudges	Make personal negative comments which destroy self-esteem, foster grudges and perpetuate a cycle of aggression.	Label the behaviour not the pupil – you value them but their behaviour is not acceptable.
Body language	Threatening body language such as finger pointing, fist waving.	Relaxed body language conveys confidence and sets clear intentions.
Ultimatums	Ultimatums are issued which are unrealistic or impossible to implement. The pupil is given no room for manoeuvre and is put on the spot.	Ultimatums can represent a last resort and are only issued if the member of staff is sure they can be implemented. They provide exits, offer choices and/or resolution.
Humour	There is no humour evident and emotion is exposed through embarrassment or unfavourable comparison with pupils.	Humour is introduced into the situation but not at the expense of the pupil conveying difficulties.
Right of reply	The pupil has no right of reply and is aggressive on account of being compelled to be silent.	There is a tone of expectation of compliance but skilfully the pupil is invited to offer their views.

Examining the various styles of resolving conflict and deciding which one to use and whether or not it is effective could be the starting point of developing strategies that are likely to assist in the de-escalation of conflicts and have an impact on daily routines. Staff are able to help pupils develop and employ a wide range of strategies enabling them to have a real choice about their behaviour. In perceiving conflict as positive staff experience less stress, are good role models, acquire skills for dealing with conflict within and outside school and create opportunities for pupils to practise skills in a non-threatening environment. Their pupils acquire significant social skills and are both models and resources for others. Staff can actively encourage a desire to find solutions and pupils can learn to ask for help from staff and each other. What is essential is that in order to develop conflict resolution skills they need to be practised by both staff and pupils. Many of the exercises in this book provide a vehicle for coming at a problem from a variety of angles, engaging in debate and arriving at conclusions – albeit sometimes agreeing to disagree.

Skilled interventions: a graduated intervention plan

Coming to agreement about what exactly constitutes disruption is not always easy for classroom practitioners and attempts to itemise specific behaviours often arrive at conclusions that reveal how relatively low level disruption can have a major impact on classroom climate. The Elton Report (DES, 1989) underlined that a major issue for teachers was usually disruption of the lesson caused by behaviour such as talking out of turn and making unnecessary noises. Despite occasional media grabbing headlines on violence, teachers continue to report that interruptions to learning remain their main concern. Verbal abuse towards teachers was reported less frequently than hindering other pupils and other forms of disruption to the lesson (Charlton and David, 1993).

The skilled professional in a classroom context draws upon a variety of graduated strategies which move from minimal intrusion through to intervention necessary to secure conclusion of the problem. These stages may not be as clearly defined as stated here but it is important that staff differentiate between them and provide clarity of direction. The advantage of such an approach is that it offers alternatives should the initial action prove unsuccessful. Sometimes, in cases where personal safety is threatened, such considered response may be abandoned but these are usually rare moments.

1 **Initial interventions** deal with minor issues that are low level. They are the ones that often provide an erosion of order in the classroom and can be stressful.

2 **Further interventions** will be necessary when certain pupils demonstrate that the initial response has not been totally successful.

3 **Final interventions**, which are often the most intrusive and, in themselves, can be disruptive, will be required if pupils are still finding it difficult to come to terms with the required changes in their own behaviour. Sometimes it is the case that these are the *initial* responses of adults and they leave no further avenue to explore if they fail.

Ten steps to discipline

One of the key influences on contemporary behaviour management and the idea of a hierarchy of responses to negative behaviour in the classroom is William Glasser (1969). He declares that effective classroom management is not easy but one attribute is essential – consistency. His discipline plan (SDE 6.1) is broader in sweep but nonetheless offers significant points for reflection. It starts with self-analysis, moves into engagement with the pupil and concludes with isolation and exclusion. Solution finding, rule reminders and catching pupils being good all feature in the plan, but it is the emphasis on teachers taking a reflective look at their own practice first that provides the initial platform for engagement.

Responses to disruption

Over thirty years ago Hargreaves et al. (1975) researched and listed the range of ways in which teachers were found to respond to initial disruption. They were:

- stating or restating the rule

- appealing to pupil's knowledge of the rule

- command /request for conformity

- prohibition

- questions about the behaviour

- statement of consequences of negative behaviour

- warnings and threats

- judgemental labels

- sarcasm

- attention grabbers.

Despite its date, the breadth of forms of response are unlikely to have changed a great deal and it has been suggested in more recent work that the most frequent teacher comments are the short 'shut up' or 'stop it' (Watkins and Wagner, 2004). Harsh, sudden and negative statement are required in emergency situations when the adult perceives danger or extreme threat, but as a dominant, initial response to relatively low level negativity they appear either authoritarian or the opposite and therefore lack any real control.

STAFF DEVELOPMENT EXERCISE
SDE 6.1 TEN STEPS TO DISCIPLINE

a Read through Ten Steps and reflect on your own practice and, where appropriate, recent classroom management issues.

b In small groups, examine the value of the Ten Steps in the classroom and devise a similar plan on intervention that could be added to the behaviour policy based upon initial, further and final interventions.

Step	Comments and questions
1: Self-analysis	Ask yourself, 'what am I doing?', 'how do I react when pupils misbehave?', 'do I shout, threaten, exclude, ignore?'
2: Failing techniques	Ask also, 'is it working?' If the answer is 'no' then stop doing it! Sometimes we continue with approaches that are not making any difference to pupil behaviour and classroom climate.
3: Positive reinforcement	'Catch them being good' when they are not misbehaving or give them some form of recognition when they are on task. This gives the message that they are noticed and you can be pleasant as well as firm.
4: Early intervention	If the pupil disrupts respond by saying, 'what are you doing?', sharply but not angrily. Don't say things such as 'stop it' or 'don't do that'.
5: Rule reminder	If disruption continues repeat step 4 and add, 'it is against the rules.' If there is no response, say, 'this is what I saw you doing, it is against the rules'.
6: Solution finding	If disruption continues say, 'we have got to work this out', then find a solution whereby the pupil follows reasonable rules and does not disrupt others. 'This cannot go on. We have got to work it out'.
7: Isolation in class	If no solution is found then the pupil should be withdrawn from the group and placed on their own within the classroom until a solution for being part of the group is worked out.
8: Isolation out of class	If it continues they should be sent from the room to a designated place in the school. They must 'work it out' before being allowed to return.
9: Isolation out of school	If this is refused the student must be sent home and parents told that they are unwilling to work out a way of fitting in with school rules.
10: Outside agencies	If parents report they cannot deal with their child then outside agencies will be needed.

STAFF DEVELOPMENT EXERCISE

SDE 6.2 INITIAL RESPONSES

Examine the list of initial responses to troublesome behaviour. In the final column indicate through scaling (1 being least desirable, 10 most desirable) which intervention would be your desired responses and then reflect on which responses you find yourself using most. Share your thoughts with your colleagues in small groups.

Intervention	Example	Scale 1–10
Describing the negative behaviour	'You have not had permission to leave your seat.' 'It has taken you a long time to start work.'	
Stating or restating the rule	'Walk in the classroom.' 'Two at a time when using the sink.'	
Appealing to pupil's knowledge of the rule	'You know what the rule is about respecting equipment.' 'Remember the listening rule when I am reading the story.'	
Command/demand obedience	'Quiet now everyone.' 'You must turn around now.'	
Prohibitions	'Stop it now.' 'Don't you dare do that in this classroom.'	
Questions	'What should you be doing now?' 'Did you hear what I said?'	
Statement of consequences of behaviour	'Unless you are all quiet I will not turn on the television.' 'You need to calm down or you won't be able to join us in the next activity.'	
Warnings and threats	'You'll be sent to time out.' 'I'll be telling your mother about this.'	
Judgemental labels	'Stop being an idiot!' 'You plonker!'	
Sarcasm	'That was very bright of you.' 'You'll go a long way with that kind of behaviour.'	
Attention grabbers	'Year 6!' 'You lot!'	

The following ideas on intervention techniques are approaches to specific problems but seeing them as just techniques is narrow. They form part of a designed, rehearsed and shared way to respond to misbehaviours in the classroom and maybe other school settings and benefit by being discussed as part of staff development and transforming policy to practice. Teaching assistants, support staff and teachers will benefit through knowing how colleagues respond and what they respond to. Suggested ideas are not attempts to stifle originality or prevent individual teaching styles being developed, nor are they prescriptive in the sense that they are the only ways of responding. They are simply illustrations of ideas that merit attention. What they illustrate is that the emotional climate in a classroom does not have to substantively change because one or maybe several pupils decide to react negatively and that theory can transform into practice that supports the generation of order in the classroom. What must be emphasised is that whatever techniques staff apply, they can only complement or enhance the relationship with pupils and they are not a substitute for it.

STAFF DEVELOPMENT EXERCISE

SDE: 6.3 SELF-EVALUATION: CLASSROOM MANAGEMENT SKILLS

It is important to consider your own responses to disruption and to engage in a piece of self-reflection before reading through the suggestions in the rest of the chapter. You may wish to refer back to SDE 5.1 and how you replied or might have replied to those questions. It may also be helpful to share the outcomes, or part of them, with members of your team.

Question	Self-evaluation comments
What about your body language conveys confidence?	
What about the tone of your voice conveys confidence?	
What are your initial responses to a behaviour problem in the classroom?	
What are your further responses to a behaviour problem in the classroom?	
What are your final responses to a behaviour problem in the classroom?	

Initial intervention stage: minimal interference

Initial verbal instructions should be kept to a minimum and be non-intrusive. On the other hand the significance of non-verbal aspects of effective behaviour management cannot be overstated. Noticing behaviour that is potentially disruptive may lead to a choice to take *no action at all* but to observe events closely as any intervention potentially draws more attention to the behaviour and can in itself be disruptive – more disruptive than what is happening!

The effect of body language is crucial as it can convey confidence but it can also be a betrayal when what is spoken is open and caring but what is conveyed by body language is something different. One of the betrayers is pointing a finger which is hard to do without being accusatory. On the other hand an 'open hand' gesture can emphasise effectively but without the accompanying severity. Part of minimising the verbal intrusion is to ensure that the agreed rules and, if possible, lesson plan are visible and referred to. As stated before there is no point in publishing rules if no reference is made to them and they do help in diffusing situations. Sometimes simply standing next to the emerging disruptive pupil and highlighting the relevant section can serve as a reminder.

'Proximity control', or moving closer the pupil who is beginning to misbehave, can be effective as an interception before escalation. There are times when, as part of a planned intervention, a member of staff might move closer to a pupil who is starting to exhibit lack of motivation and is off task. However, it is a technique that may have the opposite effect when a pupil is angry and that anger is directed at you or other authority figures, or when making demands on pupils who often function better away from authority figures. One way of talking closely to a pupil in the escalation or de-escalation phases of anger (Faupel et al., 1998) is to stand at the side, which almost negates eye contact and any misreading of body language.

When there is demand for verbal instruction it is worth considering that both high volume and high tone are likely to be indicators of stress. The adult voice should be clear and lower in tone than usual. This gives a message of:

- expectation of compliance

- calmness and control

- non-engagement with any emotional agenda.

If pupils continue to be defiant, the 'broken record', which is a continual, calm repetition of the instruction, can be tried. Words such as 'should', 'must' or 'ought' and their negative counterparts are difficult to use without sounding as if it is a lecture and they often form part of what turns into an unhelpful monologue rather than a brief rule reminder. Offering a description of the negative behaviour, for example 'you are out your seat', can be emotionally neutral, as can simple, straightforward rule reminders, and the use of consequences places the onus on the pupil to take some responsibility for what will happen next. Allowing the pupil time to absorb instruction and for your request or instruction to be taken up is often referred to as 'take up time' and is a useful skill. Once again it conveys calmness. The alternative, requiring immediate action, will usually require a raised voice and a shouted 'now'.

'You're talking when you shouldn't be – quiet NOW'

or

'You're talking during silent work time – make sure you are back on task
after I have seen Jack.'

Further intervention

In all aspects of classroom management it is essential to transmit an expectation of compliance. An instruction or a request should be followed by 'thanks', which conveys that
your request *will be* carried out and you are thanking the pupils for it. 'Please', especially
if repeated many times, can appear as a plea for compliance. 'Thanks' is assertive whereas
the constantly reiterated 'please' can almost sound passive aggressive (page 89). Similarly,
avoid a negative element in a positive comment, since pupils may 'biased scan' and only
hear the negative, thereby diminishing all that has gone before or the intention to praise
or celebrate. Pupils with low self-esteem usually pick up those parts which confirm their
feelings about themselves. Such statements often begin with 'if only', 'but' or 'why'.

'You have tried hard – there are a couple of spellings we need to sort out
but it is going well and you have shown how careful you are with your project work.'

is better than

'Nice drawing but too many mistakes in the writing.'

or

'If only you would sit in your seat we would all be happier.'

or

'Look how much you have done – great – why don't you do that all the time.'

One of the hardest threats that disruption poses is that it can escalate emotionally and
spiral into a breakdown of the lesson. One helpful way to avoid this is to concentrate on
the initial disruptive behaviour staying focused upon the 'primary' behaviour (Rogers,
1995) and not allowing 'secondary' behaviours to be brought onto the agenda. Staff can
easily become distracted and the reaction of the pupil to the original instruction and the
initial cause of the problem remain unresolved.

Two reactions that frequently occur are 'I don't care' and a semi-belligerent, half question 'why'. Associated with the teenage years, but often heard in younger pupils, 'I don't
care' is designed as a final statement (see below) and a forced end to your involvement.
Reframing and agreeing with an 'I don't care' statement can help if followed by a consequence or reason statement and also invoking the good of the group by linking your
request or sanction to a need to maintain the impetus of the lesson and group welfare.

'I'm glad you do not mind as I have to enforce the rule to make sure that
the class keep on task.'

In demanding reasons pupils seek to control the situation, gain attention and fluster the adult by perpetually saying 'why' – 'why do I have to do this?', 'why do we have this rule?' Rather than resort to an authority position by giving answers suggesting that they must comply because you say so, it may be better to deflect the issue by agreeing to discuss the issues and provide answers during a break, when the tension and importance of the issue may be less intense. Try to ask 'where' and 'when' questions instead of giving direct orders which often invite the 'why' response.

> 'When did I say we would move to the next item?'

> 'Where were you meant to be sitting, Tariq?'

When disruption indicates a need for attention, one way of handling this is not to directly respond to exhibited behaviours but to meet the pupil's attention needs by noticing them. Attention seeking may be diffused by a small injection of attention and affection or alternatively by accepting the idea that behaviour is goal led and allowing the goal to be revealed.

> 'Jenny, that looks like a good start.'

> 'Liam, your homework was good.'

> 'You appear to want my attention and not allow others to work.'

Difficult pupils, especially older ones who experience a variety of subject teachers, sometimes play staff off against each other by suggesting that certain behaviours that are unacceptable in your class are not regarded as such by your colleagues: 'Mr. Jones doesn't care if I bite the ruler'. Consistent enforcement of rules helps neutralise such a response as some pupils will use inconsistency to their advantage. After a brief 'thank you' emphasise that your request is simply linked to the agreed class/school rules – that one published on the board about respect for property – and not connected with particular staff.

Final interventions

Outright refusal to comply and wanting the last word means that the final intervention stage has been reached. The pupil expresses the idea that they cannot be made to do what you tell them, which is probably true, and they are threatening the lesson and inviting your emotionally charged attempts to control them, which they will then ridicule. This may be resolved by taking the aggression out of the situation through agreement, adding that they are the only person who can control themselves and that you trust they will make the right decision and accept the subsequent consequences. However, you might find yourself becoming hooked into a debate as both you and the pupil seek to have the last word, which means that the winner will have seemingly asserted their dominance. The last word is not the winner, so let the pupil have it and, if you feel it will be productive, reconsider their behaviour with them at another time, although the chances are that the 'heat' will have died down.

Out of the classroom In any consideration of final interventions it is important to mention the practice of pupils being told to leave the classroom whether as punishment, sanction or consequence as it illustrates an extreme reaction from staff and the degree to which certain behaviours or pupils can impact upon lessons. There are times when the emotional climate in a classroom becomes so charged that staff have to resort to separating pupils from each other or from themselves. That avenue must remain open for staff and there is no intention here to deny it. Some lessons would be destroyed if the exit route were not used. Nonetheless, the drawbacks of pupils spending prolonged periods outside of class and especially away from opportunities to talk with adults need to be underlined and sending a pupil out should be a final course of action not an immediate response. Roger's (2004) notion of a discipline plan moves from *least* intrusive to *most* intrusive and might see exit from the room as a final step. There are four arguments that require reflection.

■ There is a danger that being outside the classroom becomes a norm for many pupils and it ends up confirming their view of themselves as being of little worth. Alternatively, it may provide an opportunity to meet other pupils who have similarly been sent out as part of a pre-arrangement.

■ Should the occasions spent outside begin to increase, it is likely to confirm the idea that increasing punishments or sanctions in number, severity or both has very little impact on the likelihood of misbehaviour recurring.

■ The importance of the balance between positive and negative is discussed elsewhere but it is impossible to catch the pupil being good if they are persistently outside the room.

■ Unless the lesson concludes with the pupil in the room, restoration and explanation of the link of the sanction to the rules cannot take place which invites the pupil to take up where they left off during the next lesson.

School policies need to explore 'time-out' arrangements, how they are monitored, how effective they are in dealing with pupil behaviour and how they enhance staff skills. In addition, attention needs to be paid to the restitution phase and how staff will re-establish the relationship. No matter how skilled the intervention, occasional damage to the staff–pupil relationship, so carefully built up over the year, occurs and there is a need to reaffirm it without losing authority. This should be done as soon as possible through such actions as a cursory but timely enquiry about progress in work which deflects from behaviour matters and reorientates the relationship to what really matters – learning.

At the end of this chapter you will have decided what your approach is to:

■ assertiveness and conflict as positive classroom forces

■ graduated approaches to dealing with disruption

■ the initial phase in dealing with interruptions to learning

■ any further action that you might take

■ the final actions required should the first two stages not prove successful.

Some final thoughts

In the belief, and it may be true, that certain schools are reacting to what is believed to be increasing discipline problems with 'zero-tolerance' and 'get tough' policies (Arum, 2003: 194) it is essential to ask what difference they really make to the school climate. These draconian approaches serve the needs of some staff, usually those who are already and always have been operating in this way and want to demonstrate to outside authorities that they are *wrestling* with the problem (*wrestling* – big, muscular fighters running around a ring until the preordained result is achieved but little has really happened and nothing really changed). The message to their colleagues is twofold: either (a) be like me and all will be resolved or (b) you are hopeless – let me show you how it is done. What 'get tough' often means is 'get aggressive', not be assertive, consistent, imaginative, supportive and collaborative. It harks back to a tradition of obedience without question and 'do what I tell you', not 'do what is right' or 'do what is wise'.

In Chapter 4 the issue of who owns the power in classrooms was discussed with emphasis on the power of the pupil. Now it is time to redress that balance and purvey another view or make another argument. Authority appears to be questioned and challenged in a variety of arenas in modern society and it would be hard to imagine that schools are immune from those challenges. Obedience based upon authority is less likely to work and there appears to have been a shift from 'I have the right to teach you' to 'you have the right to learn and I have the skills to teach you'. Teaching and supporting pupil development needs a new power and it is arriving through professional development. In many respects power still rests with adults but it has shifted from being power based upon authority and exercised through authoritarian approaches to power based upon the knowledge, skills and ideas that inform the professional classroom. In terms of behaviour management, new practices emerge from staff becoming involved in researching their practices, reflecting on what works, considering the findings of others and sharing new found skills in collaborative cultures. The growing engagement of professionals in enhancing their knowledge through post-qualification study for teachers and foundation degrees for support staff means that staff are wiser and working more smartly – 'get smart not tough'. Professional development in a school culture which welcomes new ideas and challenges and acknowledges that learning about teaching is a lifelong journey leads to a new empowerment, not based on the position teachers and other adults occupy in schools, but on new and improved ways of working.

What is described above is positive and endorsement of the search to find solutions to problems that have existed in schools probably since schooling began. They certainly have been present for over 70 years if Waller's view of schools is accurate.

> School ... is a despotism threatened from within and exposed to regulation and interference from without. It is a despotism demanded by the community of parents, but specially limited by them as to the techniques which it may use for the maintenance of a stable social order.
>
> (Waller, 1932)

Throughout this book much has been made of rewards, enhancing skills, sanctions, theoretical underpinning and specific techniques – all of which are essential to a well-tuned behaviour management policy. They are also crucial elements in developing relationships with pupils, especially those who present consistently challenging behaviours, and it is those relationships that are pivotal to success (Lines, 2003). Easily damaged, difficult to build and constantly threatened, it is the fragile relationship with pupils that will provide the greatest opportunity for success in changing behaviour.

The call in this book for enhanced skills based on research and reflection is not simply directed at individual teaching assistants or teachers. A school cannot afford staff, however skilful, operating individually and idiosyncratically when the chance to share ideas and practice is available. Rogers (1995) emphasises the value of:

- unity over isolation

- reflection over impulse

- communication over mere expectation

- collaboration over private practice.

Becoming united, collaborative and reflective is enhanced by sharing views, trading opinions, and engaging in arguments and positive conflict on the journey towards a consensus that has the behaviour policy as its tangible expression. This book was designed to inform and structure that experience with the aim of stimulating debate and discussion, informing policy and practice, and, ultimately, benefiting pupils. I hope it has gone some way towards that.

Appendix: Planning sheet for Staff Development Exercises

SDE	Page	Exercise title	Time*	Tick
1.1	3	What is a behaviour policy?	30	
1.2	6	The policy framework	45	
1.3	16	Evaluation of the current system	30	
1.4	18	Major statements	20	
1.5	19	Indicators of the school ethos	30	
2.1	30	Individual or solution focused theory	20	
3.1	38	Guidelines for reviewing rules	30	
3.2	40	Audit of classroom rules	20	
3.3	43	Praise versus encouragement	30	
3.4	46	Rewards are bribes or are natural	20	
3.5	48	Rewards in my school	15	
3.6	52	Rank ordering effective rewards	20	
4.1	56	Power in schools	30	
4.2	61	Clarifying thoughts and beliefs on punishment	20	
4.3	62	Effective punishment	20	
4.4	68	Considering consequences	20	
4.5	72	Restorative reflections	15	
5.1	76	Precious and not so precious memories	30	
5.2	79	Self-evaluation: presence	20	
5.3	82	Advice for new staff at the beginning of the job	15	
5.4	84	To line up or not to line up	20	
6.1	93	Tens steps to discipline	20	
6.2	94	Initial responses	20	
6.3	96	Self-evaluation: classroom management skills	30	

* The times are approximate minutes per exercise. They will vary considerably and initial SDEs will indicate whether these times are generous, not sufficient or even about right!

Bibliography

Algozzine, B. and White, R. (2002) 'Preventing Problem Behaviours Using Schoolwide Discipline', in B. Algozzine and P. Kay, *Preventing Problem Behaviours: a Handbook of Successful Prevention Strategies*. California, USA: Corwin Press.

Allen, B., Robinson, G. and Maines, B. (1994) *If it makes my life easier to write a policy*. Bristol: Lame Duck Publishing.

Arum, R. (2003) *Judging School Discipline: the Crisis of Moral Authority*. Massachusetts, USA: Harvard University Press.

Ayers, H., Clarke, D. and Murray, A. (1995) *Perspectives on Behaviour: A Practical Guide to Effective Interventions for Teachers*. London: David Fulton.

Ayres, H. and Gray, F. (1998) *Classroom Management: A Practical Approach for Primary and Secondary Teachers*. London: David Fulton.

Barrow, G. (1998) 'Perspectives on Behaviour: Theory and Examples', in *Disaffection and Inclusion: Merton's Mainstream Approach to Difficult Behaviour*. Bristol: Centre for Studies on Inclusive Education. pp. 27–32.

Barrow, G., Bradshaw, E. and Newton, T. (2001) *Improving Behaviour and Raising Self-esteem in the Classroom: a Practical Guide to Using Transactional Analysis*. London: David Fulton.

Behaviour4Learning (2005) *Behaviour and Attendance Materials for Primary Initial Teacher Training Tutors*. Nottingham: (IPRN) for Behaviour4Learning.

Behaviour4Learning (2006) *Behaviour and Attendance Materials for Secondary Initial Teacher Training Tutors*. Nottingham: (IPRN) for Behaviour4Learning.

Brandes, D. and Ginnis, P. (1990) *The Student-Centred School*. Hemel Hempstead: Simon and Schuster Education.

Canter, L. and Canter, M. (2001) *Assertive Discipline*, 3rd edn. Los Angeles: Canter and Associates.

Chaplain, R. (2003) *Teaching Without Disruption: a Model for Managing Pupil Behaviour*. London: RoutledgeFalmer.

Charlton, T. and David, K. (1993) *Managing Misbehaviour in Schools*. London: Routledge.

Cooper, P. and Upton, G. (1990) 'Turning Conflict into Co-operation: An Ecosystemic Approach to Interpersonal Conflict and its Relevance to Pastoral Care in Schools', *Pastoral Care in Education*, 7 (4): 10–15.

Cornwall, J. (2004) 'Pressure, Stress and Children's Behaviour at School' in J. Wearmouth, T. Glyn, R. Richmond and M. Berryman, *Understanding Pupil Behaviour in Schools: a Diversity of Approaches*. London: David Fulton.

Corrie, L. (2002) *Investigating Troublesome Classroom Behaviour: Practical Tools for Teachers*. London: RoutledgeFalmer.

Department of Education and Science (DES) (1989) *Discipline in Schools – Report of the Committee of Enquiry: The Elton Report*, 12: 3. London: HMSO.

Department for Education and Science (DfES) (2004) *Key Stage 3 National Strategy: Advice on Whole School Behaviour and Attendance Policy*. London: DfES.

De Shazer, S. (1985) *Keys to Solution in Brief Therapy*. New York: W. W. Norton and Co.

Dobson, J. (2003) *The New Dare to Discipline*. Illinois, USA: Tyndale House Publishers.

Dreikurs, R. (1968) *Psychology in the Classroom: a Manual for Teachers*, 2nd edn. New York: Harper and Row.

Dreikurs, R. and Cassel, P. (1990) *Discipline Without Tears: What to Do with Children who Misbehave*, 2nd edn. New York: Dutton.

Dreikurs, R., Grunwald, B. and Pepper, F. (1998) *Maintaining Sanity in the Classroom: Classroom Management Techniques*, 2nd edn. Philadelphia: Taylor and Francis.

Faupel, A., Herrick, E. and Sharp, P. (1998) *Anger Management: a Practical Guide*. London: David Fulton.

Glasser, W. (1969) *Schools Without Failure*. New York: Peter H. Wyden Publishing.

Glasser, W. (1992) *The Quality School: Managing Students without Coercion*. New York: Harper Collins.

Gordon, G. (1996) *Managing Challenging Children*. Nuneaton: Prim-Ed Publishing.

Gordon, T. (1974) *Teacher Effectiveness Training*. New York: Peter H. Wyden Publishing.

Hall, C. and Hornby, G. (2003) *Learning to Collaborate: Working Across the Divide in Counselling Pupils in Schools: Skills and Strategies for Teachers*. London: RoutledgeFalmer.

Hargreaves, D., Hester, K. and Mellor, J. (1975) *Deviance in Classrooms*. London: Routledge and Kegan Paul.

Harris, T. (1969) *I'm OK – You're OK*: a Practical Guide to Transactional Analysis. New York: Harper and Row.

Harrop, A. and Williams, T. (1992) 'Rewards and punishments in the primary school: pupils' perceptions and teachers' usage', *Educational Psychology*, 7 (4): 211–15.

Hill, F. and Parsons, L. (2000) *Teamwork in the Management of Emotional and Behavioural Difficulties*. London: David Fulton.

Hook, P. and Vaas, A. (2000), *Creating Winning Classrooms*. London: David Fulton.

Hopkins, B. (2002) 'Restorative Justice in Schools', *Support for Learning*, 17 (3): 144–9.

Jenks, C. (1996) *Childhood*. Routledge: London.

Kinder, K. and Wilkin, A. (1996) *Disaffection: What are effective school-based strategies?* NFER: unpublished research paper: BERA: Lancaster.

Klein, R. (1999) *Defying Disaffection*. Stoke-on-Trent: Trentham Books.

Kohn, A. (2001) *Beyond Discipline: From Compliance to Community*. New Jersey, USA: Merrill Prentice-Hall.

Lawrence, J., Steed, D. and Young, P. (1984) 'European voices on disruptive behaviour in schools: definitions, concerns and types of behaviour', *British Journal of Educational Studies*, 32 (1): 4–17.

Leaman, L. (2006) *Classroom Confidential*. London: Continuum Publishing.

Lee, C. (2004) *Preventing Bullying in Schools*. London: Paul Chapman Publishing.

Lee, C. (2006) 'Exploring Teachers' Definitions of Bullying', *Emotional and Behavioural Difficulties*, 11 (1): 61–75.

Lines, D. (2003) 'Insights into the Management of Challenging Behaviour in Schools', *Pastoral Care in Education*, 21 (1): 26–35.

MacGrath, M. (2000) *The Art of Peaceful Teaching in the Primary School*. London: David Fulton.

Macleod, G. (2006) 'Bad, mad or sad: constructions of young people in trouble and implications for interventions', *Emotional and Behavioural Difficulties*, 11 (3): 155–67.

McLean, A. (2003) *The Motivated School*. London: Paul Chapman Publishing.

McManus, M. (1995) *Troublesome Behaviour in the Classroom*, 2nd edn. London: Routledge.

McNamara, E. (1999) *Positive Pupil Management and Motivation: A Secondary Teacher's Guide*. London: David Fulton.

Merrett, F. and Wheldall, K. (1984) 'Classroom Behaviour Problems which Junior School Teachers Say They Find Most Troublesome', *Educational Review*, 40: 13–27.

Molnar, A. and Lindquist, B. (1990) *Changing Problem Behaviour in Schools*. San Francisco: Jossey-Bass.

Neill, A. S. (1968) *Summerhill*. Middlesex: Penguin Books.

Office for Standards in Education (Ofsted) (2001) *Improving Attendance and Behaviour in Secondary Schools*. London: HMI.

Olsen, J. and Cooper, P. (2001) *Dealing with Disruptive Students in the Classroom*. London: Kogan Page.

Pikas, A. (1989) 'The Common Concern Method for the Treatment of Mobbing', in E. Roland and E. Munthe (eds) *Bullying: an International Perspective*. London: David Fulton.

Porter, L. (2000) *Behaviour In Schools: Theory and Practice for Teachers*. Berkshire: Open University Press.

Rhodes, J. and Ajmal, Y. (1995) *Solution Focused Thinking in Schools: Behaviour, Reading and Organisation*. London: BT Press.

Riddall-Leech, S. (2003) *Managing Children's Behaviour*. Oxford: Heinemann.

Robinson, G. and Maines, B. (1997) *Crying for Help: the No Blame Approach to Bullying*. Bristol: Lucky Duck Publishing.

Rogers, B. (1990) *You Know the Fair Rule: Strategies for Making the Hard Job of Discipline in School Easier*. Harlow: Longman.

Rogers, B. (1995) *Behaviour Management: a Whole School Approach*. London: Paul Chapman Publishing.

Rogers, B. (2002) *Establishment Phase: Practice and Skills*. Unpublished paper.

Rogers, B. (2004) 'The Language of Behaviour Management', in J. Wearmouth, R. Richmond and T. Glynn, *Addressing Pupils' Behaviour: Responses at District, School and Individual Levels*. London: David Fulton.

Rutter, M., Maughan, B., Mortimore, P., Ouston, J. and Smith, A. (1979) *Fifteen Thousand Hours*. London: Open Books.

Scottish Office (1992) *Using Ethos Indicators in Secondary School Self Evaluation*. Scottish Office Education Department (SOED) .

Sharp, S. and Smith, P. (1994) *Tackling Bullying in Your School*. London: Routledge.

Tankersley, M., Landrum, T. and Cook, B. (2004) 'How Research Informs Practice in the Field of Emotional and Behavioural Disorders', in R. Rutherford, M. Magee Quinn and S. Mathur, *Handbook of Research in Emotional and Behavioural Disorders*. New York: The Guilford Press.

Tyler, K. and Jones, B. (2002) 'Teachers' Responses to the Ecosystemic Approach to Changing Chronic Problem Behaviour in School', *Pastoral Care in Education*, 20 (2): 30–9.

Upton, G. and Cooper, P. (1990) 'A New Perspective on Behaviour Problems in Schools: The Ecosystemic Approach', *Maladjustment and Therapeutic Education*, 1: 3–18.

Visser, J. (2000) *Managing Behaviour in Classrooms*. London, David Fulton.

Waller, W. (1932) *The Sociology of Teaching*. New York: John Wiley and Sons.

Watkins, C. and Wagner, P. (2004) 'Improving Classroom Behaviour', in J. Wearmouth, R. Richmond and T. Glynn, *Addressing Pupils' Behaviour: Responses at District, School and Individual Levels*. London: David Fulton.

Wearmouth, J. (1997) 'Pygmalion Lives On', *Support for Learning*, 12 (3): 20–5.

Wheeler, S. (1996) 'Behaviour Management: Rewards or Sanctions', *Journal Of Teacher Development*, 5 (1): 51–5.

Wilson, J. (2002) 'Punishment and Pastoral Care', *Pastoral Care in Education*, 20 (1): 25–9.

Wolfgang, C. (2005) *Solving Discipline and Classroom Management Problems: Methods and Models for Today's Teachers*, 6th edn. New Jersey, USA: John Wiley.

Wragg, E. (ed) (1984) *Classroom Teaching Skills*. London: Croom Helm.

Wragg, E. (1993) *Classroom Management*. London: Routledge.

Wright, D. (2005) *There's no need to shout: the Secondary Teacher's Guide to Successful Behaviour Management*. Cheltenham: Nelson Thornes.

Young, M. (1992) *Counselling Methods and Techniques: an Eclectic Approach*. New York: Merrill.

Zehr, H. (1990) *Changing Lenses: a New Focus for Crime and Justice*. Scottdale, PA: Herald.

Websites

www.luckyduck.co.uk

Index